PENGUIN BOOKS

ROALD DAHL'S COOKBOOK

Roald Dahl's parents were Norwegian, but he was born in Llandaff, Wales, in 1916, and educated at Repton School. At the outbreak of the Second World War, he enlisted in the RAF in Nairobi. His first short stories were based on his wartime experiences. He was one of the most successful and well known of all children's writers. He died in November 1990. *The Times* described him as 'one of the most widely read and influential writers of our generation … Children loved his stories and made him their favourite … Some believe that they will be classics of the future.'

Felicity Dahl was born in Llandaff, Wales. When she was nineteen she worked in the fashion department of *Harper's Bazaar* and a couple of years later she joined Scenery Limited as a freelance stylist for television commercials. She attended a Carving and Guilding course at the City and Guilds London Art School and in 1981 she and others started their own business, Carvers and Guilders. With three daughters from a previous marriage, Felicity married Roald Dahl in 1983. She lives at Gipsy House, the family home in Great Missenden, Buckinghamshire.

# Felicity &
# Roald Dahl

# Roald Dahl's
# Cookbook

*Photographs by Jan Baldwin*

PENGUIN BOOKS

PENGUIN BOOKS

Published by the Penguin Group
Penguin Books Ltd, 27 Wrights Lane, London W8 5TZ, England
Penguin Books USA Inc., 375 Hudson Street, New York, New York 10014, USA
Penguin Books Australia Ltd, Ringwood, Victoria, Australia
Penguin Books Canada Ltd, 10 Alcorn Avenue, Toronto, Ontario, Canada M4V 3B2
Penguin Books (NZ) Ltd, 182–190 Wairau Road, Auckland 10, New Zealand

Penguin Books Ltd, Registered Offices: Harmondsworth, Middlesex, England

First published by Viking under the title *Memories with Food At Gipsy House* 1991
Published in Penguin Books, with minor revisions, under the present title 1996
1 3 5 7 9 10 8 6 4 2

Printed in Italy by Lego spa - Vicenza

*For Lorina*

14 March 1963 – 25 March 1990

*'Not many who found her were*
*able to let her go.'*
Charles Sturridge

# CONTENTS

The Family Tree —and

Harald Dahl    Sophie Magdalene Hesselberg
Mormor

Alf

Roald

Else    Asta

Atty

Tessa      Theo   Ophelia     Lucy

Sophie
Clover
Luke

Phoebe
Chloë

Jan

ther characters in this book

Alphonsus Ligori          Elizabeth d'Abreu
        Pon                      Betty

clare            Liccy            Spiv

Neisha      Cha-cha      Loopy

and  Josie

# FOREWORD

On 23 November 1990 Roald died. During the last year of his life, in between bouts of illness, he worked with me on this book and a Diary for children. Both books open a window into his life that will probably surprise many of you. His family meant everything to him. This was surely the influence of his remarkable mother, known as Mama. Roald's short tribute to her in this book says it all.

This huge and wonderful man showed boundless kindness to others. To me he was the greatest husband a woman could ever have. To all our children he was the greatest father and friend, and to so many children round the world the greatest writer. I hope the book we have written gives to you and your family a feast both to read and to eat.

My sister Spiv and her husband Marius have captured the essence of this book in a tribute to Roald published in the *Independent*.

'"Treats!" he would cry, displaying a dinner table laden with quantities of his favourite food: Norwegian prawns, or lobster, or caviar or scrumptious roast beef. Second and third helpings were pressed on his lucky guests. With the coffee he would place on the table a grubby plastic box crammed with chocolate goodies, irresistible to dogs, children and adults alike. Excellent claret and inevitable chocolates were essential parts of his enthusiasm for food, drink and conversation.'

Like his mother, I lost a daughter and a husband within a few months. Roald and I have dedicated this to my youngest daughter Lorina who at the age of 27 died suddenly of a brain tumour on 25 March 1990.

All royalties from this book will directly benefit the Roald Dahl Foundation, the charity I established in 1991 in his memory. The Foundation gives help in three areas which profoundly affected Roald's life: haematology, neurology and literacy.

# INTRODUCTION

## Roald Dahl

A great deal of human traffic moves through Gipsy House and more than 100 suppers, not to mention lunches, are devoured here with gusto every week of the year. Liccy and I have between us six daughters, a son, two sons-in-law and five grandchildren. As well as that, we have five sisters between us, and they in their turn have their own large families of children and grandchildren. Many of this vast population live within thirty miles of Gipsy House, and all are welcome to come by for a meal. Our dining-room contains an old pine farmhouse table twelve feet long and three feet wide surrounded by many chairs, but even so there are times when it is a squash to get everyone in.

Apart from the family, there are many other visitors both for lunch and dinner, and great care is taken with the food. We are all pigs, but we are, I hope, discerning pigs who care with some passion about fine cooking. No lunch is ever eaten without a comment or a discussion or a criticism or an accolade.

This is not to say that we spend half our waking lives thinking about food, because we don't. We simply regard meals, and supper in particular, as a wonderful relaxing culmination to a day of hard work. Our suppers are times when work is forgotten and when food and wine are remembered.

The guiding genius behind all this culinary activity is my wife, Liccy, who possesses not simply a fine palate but a kind of micro-palate so sensitive it can detect the presence of a single cumin seed in a large pot of beef stew. She and I have shared many pleasures in foreign bistros and restaurants, especially in the Loire and Burgundy and Provence and the Lot, but also in Holland and Portugal and Sicily. In France we have had hundreds of superb and simple meals, nearly always in establishments that have no Michelin stars, and in southern Portugal, on a balcony overlooking a deep valley, we once had fresh Dover sole that for some reason was twice as good as any we had tasted before. These miracles happen and the moments should be savoured.

# The Cooks

The most extraordinary and eccentric of them all is Marwood Yeatman. A little later in the book you will read about how we met him and many other fascinating thoughts and recipes that Marwood himself has contributed. Look out for them.

But basically, the system at Gipsy House is this: we always have a young resident housekeeper who can drive a car and is a competent cook. She is between twenty and thirty years old and she remains with us for one year, but no longer, and is treated as part of the family. We don't want her to stay for more than a year because she has her own life and career to think about and because intelligent young girls are bound to get restless when kept in a static situation for too long a time.

These 'competent' young cooks arrive possessing varying degrees of competence. Some are already pretty damn good. Some are absolute naturals who rapidly approach virtual brilliance under Liccy's guidance, and only one in the last eight years was a slight problem at first. This last one had been carefully selected by my publishers in Australia, who had apparently forgotten to ask her about her own eating habits. She turned out to be a vegetarian. So was her mother. Neither of them had grilled a chop or a slice of bacon in her life. But Australians are a tenacious breed, and this young lady buckled down and did her job very well in the end. It was while she was walking our dogs in the afternoons that she met another young lady, called Andrea, and Andrea was married to Keith, and Keith was a gardener with exceptional skills. 'You are looking for a good gardener, aren't you?' said our Australian vegetarian to us one day. We were indeed and Keith is now with us and growing vegetables like nobody else can, thanks entirely to our charming Australian vegetarian visitor. We are ever grateful to her for that.

The other seven cooking girls were all wonderful in their different ways, and all of them finished up as fine cooks. Four of them were exceptional and one was breathtakingly brilliant, so good, in fact, that she is, apart from Liccy, the other major influence in this book. Her name is Josie Fison and there is little doubt that when she leaves us she will, with our encouragement, go on to some very serious cooking establishments to learn other aspects of the trade. Liccy is certain that Josie will finish up running some magnificent restaurant or a superb pastry-shop within a few years.

All of these girls brought unusual recipes with them when they arrived. Some invented new ones, and all of them rapidly learned to follow Liccy's instructions and occasionally even to improve upon her ideas. Each of them has her say in this book, and what she says is worth listening to. Their names are:

Lori (from Holland)
Sandy (from Australia)
Callie (from South Africa)
Virginia (from Australia)
Anne (from England)
Josie (from England)
Sarah (from England)

Others who have contributed to this book are my sisters and Liccy's sisters and a number of very carefully selected friends who have one or more recipes that are, in Liccy's opinion, outstanding.

*Clockwise, from top left:*
*Marwood Yeatman;*
*Norwegian ice-cream churn;*
*Josie Fison;*
*Gardeners and Amateurs*
*Horticultural Society Award.*

# *Liccy's Reply*

Having read my husband's glowing praises about my taste-buds, I must bring you down to earth. Firstly, I am no writer; in fact, the family know me as the illiterate one, having failed my O level in English by writing an essay on 'Hates' instead of 'Hats'. Secondly, in no way am I a professional or exceptional cook. I am, I think, a good basic cook. I possess the basic ingredients and they are, in my opinion, as follows:

1. I love food. You could call me greedy.

2. I was brought up by a mother who loved and cooked fine food. Even through those difficult war days she always managed to have something tasty on the table.

3. I love to see people enjoy their food. Like giving presents, the giver gets far more pleasure than the receiver. Having my feet under a good table with my family and friends has to be one of the happiest moments in this hard world.

4. The icing: I have a husband who voices his appreciation and positively glows during a meal I have cooked well. (We will not go into what is said when it doesn't go well.) He gives me more inspiration and incentive than anything else in my life. Love does wonders for cooking – bake in a moderate oven, turn out and it *never* fails!

I must also admit that the book would never have been published without my being the wife of this remarkable man. You might ask, 'Why has she written this book?' Well, I will tell you. One day I looked at this very long man, my husband, sitting at the head of our extraordinarily long farmhouse table, as usual, surrounded by many people all enjoying a good meal, and I realized that this was the hub of his life – this table, our family and all the funny people who join us. He dictates all his letters from this table. He reads and listens to music sitting at this table. He is interviewed at this table. He telephones from this table. The only thing he doesn't do is write at this table. It is a large part of his life, a life so full of experiences that could never have been dreamed up, even by him. So I thought a few of these moments could be recorded, along with other people's thoughts, combined with recipes that we all have enjoyed.

I must also say that this book would have been impossible without the skills of Josie. If you ever have the chance of putting your feet under *her* table, do not hesitate. Last, but by no means least, I must pay tribute to the patience and talent of Jan, whose photographs illuminate this book in such a remarkable way.

We have divided up the writing: *R.D.* is Roald, *L.D.* is Liccy. Our initials appear before each of our pieces.

# HOW TO SHOP

## Marwood Yeatman

The best buyers of food (or anything else) are opportunists. If a cook passes a shop with a hake just in, gleaming and fluffy, or a brace of partridges on the hook, he should get them first, then decide what to do with his purchase. To go out looking for either of these things could lead to disappointment, and makes no allowance for the possibility that the best fish on the slab might be haddock or herrings, that there may be no fresh fish at all, or that there might be something better in the butcher's on the way.

A serious cook goes shopping with two thoughts in mind: the number of people to feed, and the budget. Unless basics like sugar and salt are required, there is no exception to the rule. Natural food, the only proper choice, varies too much to permit any other course. It carries by far the greatest rewards, but must be examined carefully. The condition is vital. Test hams, try cheeses, and reject or keep them if necessary, like wines, until they mature. Do not encourage blanket legislation by expecting everything to be the same, and we will progress from the idea that it should.

It is important to know the places where you are likely to buy with
success. Most people think they have the best butcher, but, however
good he may be (very few are private now, anyway), there is less to
be gained from letting him choose for you than from learning to do
it for yourself, initially with his help. A good man will assist. Experts,
real experts, with nothing to hide, rarely hide much. They are only
too pleased to share their knowledge, explain why and when their
food is good, how to tell, and what to look for in a piece of pork or
rib of Devon beef.

Local specialities should be an automatic choice: the oatcakes in
Derbyshire, stotties in Durham, kippers in Craster, and shrimps,
freshly boiled on the boat, in Cley-next-the-Sea. Buy Lancashire
cheese in Preston, the hams called chaps in the Midlands, and anything else you might not recognize or find at home if you live outside
the area. Many regional foods do not travel; often, I have to collect.

Think in terms of seasons for almost *everything*. Fresh, home-
grown produce, which appears when it ought, is usually of a much
higher standard than foods made constantly available. The perfect
dinner in May or June would not, and need not, include a pheasant
and Brussels sprouts unfrozen for the occasion. It is built around
spring lamb, or lobsters, new potatoes, gooseberries, and the raw,
deep-coloured and fragrant Guernsey cream and farm butter from
cows in young grass. But, rather than looking for such things, look
forward to them and be prepared to pounce. The rest of the year,
learn to do without and compensate.

The small shops and surviving country markets in halls and sheds
(as distinct from the street) are still the best source of local and
seasonal produce. From endangered buildings and rough auctions I
have had roasting hens, boiling fowls, geese, Muscovy and tufted
duck, teal, snipe, woodcock, pigeons and rabbits galore, hares and
leverets, roe and fallow deer, salmon from the Taw, the Tamar, the
Severn, the Lune, the Wye and the Avon, sea trout, eels and every
other type of fish, trays of eggs (all sorts), black puddings, hogs'
puddings, tripe, elder, cowheel, sheep's trotters, bag, chitterlings,
apple cake, cider cake, plum cake, fat cake, heavy cake, white cake,
yellow cake, cut rounds, muffins, pikelets, parkin, bullace, damsons,
medlars, quinces, mulberries and whortleberries, filberts, sweet
chestnuts, field mushrooms, laver, salsify, samphire, scorzonera,
seakale, and baskets and baskets of garden vegetables pulled or
picked that day and good enough to win a prize at the show.

It would be unfair to take any credit for finding these things. They
merely presented themselves in countless towns and villages. All I
had to do was to keep out of a supermarket, make the most sensible
and imaginative purchase, and be careful not to ruin it when I got
home. If there are secrets to good cooking, these are three of
them.

# FIRST COURSES

Stefan's Chłodnik *22*

Chilled Cucumber and Strawberry Soup *22*

Maria's Gazpacho *23*

Almond Soup *27*

Smoked Bacon and Split Yellow Pea Soup *27*

Michael's Marvellous Medicine Chicken Soup *28*

Josie's Smokies *30*

Onion Soup *30*

Spiv's Soft Herring Roe Soufflé *32*

Herring Terrine *32*

Scandinavian Herrings *33*

Piggy's Potatoes *35*

Mussels or Clams Algarvian Style *38*

Scallop and Spinach Dainties *38*

Moules à l'Escargot *40*

Smoked Salmon Strudel *42*

Tartare of Salmon and Smoked Haddock *42*

Pike Quenelles *46*

Betty d'Abreu's Pea Dish *49*

Stilton Pâté *50*

Tomato Jelly Ring *50*

Oeufs en Gelée *54*

Callie's Quiche *56*

## Stefan's Chłodnik

*R.D.* I have been a gambler all my adult life. I can remember backing horses on the telephone way back in 1934 when I was working in the Shell Company offices in London. Having made a bet on, say, the two-o'clock race or the 2.30, I would sneak out of the office in mid-afternoon and buy an evening paper to read the latest race results in the Stop Press. In those days I was foolish enough to think I could win money by betting. Today I still gamble, but I do it purely for enjoyment and in the knowledge that I am certain to lose in the long run. I am perfectly willing to pay for my pleasure.

For the past thirty-odd years my love has been blackjack, which is little more than a slightly complex form of the family game of *vingt-et-un*, and I invariably play it in the Curzon House Club. This club owns one of the most beautiful Georgian houses in London, at 20 Curzon Street. The interior is so wonderful that it gives you a thrill just to walk into the hall, where you see the wonderful eighteenth-century screens of glass and mahogany reaching from floor to ceiling that divide the entrance hall from the staircase, and the great mahogany banisters of the staircase up which you walk to the gaming-rooms and to your doom.

This club has changed ownership at least four times while I have been there, and once, when it was owned by a very unattractive bookmaker, I was literally marched off the premises by a couple of hard men because I stood up in the dining-room and complained aloud about the quality of the food. But I was back again as soon as John Aspinall bought it and set about putting everything right. From then on, it became known as The Aspinall Curzon and it retains that name today. When the land-developer Gerald de Savary bought it from Aspinall, there were some bad moments and many of the old loyal staff disappeared. Since then, I believe, it has changed hands twice more, each time to some vast nameless conglomerate out to make a few millions in the booming property market.

Yet somehow the club itself has managed to survive, although for how long nobody knows. Perhaps by the time these words of mine are printed, it will have ceased to exist and 20 Curzon Street will have become the private home of some member of the Saudi royal family. But at the moment Liccy and I still go there once a week to dine and to play blackjack for an hour or two.*

In the old days the chef at Curzon House was an ancient Polish gentleman called Stefan. Stefan was often intoxicated, but he still managed to run the finest kitchen in town. Being of the old school, he was up every morning at 4 a.m., going to the markets to choose his own fish and vegetables. He was a lovely man, with a huge drooping moustache, and once when we went down to the kitchens to thank him for a particularly splendid meal, he was so overcome that he handed us a couple of large lobsters and insisted we take them home.

Stefan's *tour de force*, to our minds, was his chłodnik. This is a cold Polish soup with a beetroot base and a number of other special ingredients, including chunks of lobster. It is the greatest soup that I have ever tasted, ice-cold, creamy and with a flavour so subtle and enticing that you feel you want to go on eating it for ever.

*Shortly after I wrote the above, one of the richest men in Australia came into the club and won about £2,500,000. This bust them and the whole place closed down at once. So, as from July 1990, the Curzon House no longer exists as a gambling club. Where will I go now?

## Stefan's Chłodnik

Serves 6

1 lb fresh beetroots with leaves if available
about 2 pt chicken stock
1 cucumber, peeled and seeded
6 spring onions
6 radishes
1 gherkin
juice of $\frac{1}{2}$ lemon
15 fl oz sour cream
a little sugar if necessary
salt and pepper
3 tbsp chopped fresh dill

GARNISH
hard-boiled eggs, quartered
sour cream
sprigs of chopped fresh dill

1. Wash the beetroots and their leaves well, taking care not to break the skins.
2. Simmer beetroots and leaves in the chicken stock until tender. Drain, reserve the stock.
3. Peel and roughly chop the beetroots and leaves. Liquidize with the cucumber, spring onions, radishes and gherkin
4. Add $1\frac{1}{2}$ pt of stock.
5. Pass through a sieve and allow to cool.
6. When cold, add the sour cream and lemon juice, and mix well.
7. Sweeten with sugar if necessary, season to taste with salt and pepper, and add dill.
8. Chill for several hours, preferably overnight.

To serve, garnish each soup bowl with quarters of hard-boiled eggs, a whirl of sour cream and a sprig of dill. For a more luxurious garnish, add some shrimp or small pieces of cooked lobster if you are feeling rich.

## Chilled Cucumber and Strawberry Soup

PIP

Serves 4

1 large cucumber, peeled and cubed
1 oz butter
1 small onion, peeled and chopped
$1\frac{1}{4}$ pt chicken stock
1 tbsp cornflour
8 oz strawberries, finely sliced
2–3 drops food colouring (optional)
salt and freshly ground black pepper
2–3 fresh mint leaves, finely chopped
5 fl oz single cream

GARNISH
3–4 tbsp single cream
4 strawberries, finely sliced
2 tbsp chopped chives

1. Place the cubed cucumber on a clean tea towel and sprinkle with salt. Leave to drain for 30 minutes and then pat dry.
2. Soften the onion with the melted butter in a saucepan, then add the cucumber and sweat over a gentle heat for about 5 minutes.
3. Add the stock and simmer gently for about 15 minutes until the cucumber is tender.
4. Blend the cornflour with a little cold water and stir into the soup, stirring for 2–3 minutes over the heat until the soup thickens.
5. Cool and then liquidize with the strawberries (and food colouring if required). Salt and pepper to taste, add the chopped mint and, lastly, cream.
6. Chill for several hours, and remember to chill the tureen and bowls before serving.
7. Garnish with a swirl of cream, a few slices of strawberries and some chopped chives.

# Marianne Ford

*L.D.* Marianne has always been my most energetic friend. We have known each other since we were seventeen and almost immediately and simultaneously both launched into the world of fashion and photography, I with *Harper's Bazaar* and she in a photographer's studio. After a few years Marianne formed a company named Scenery, the first freelance stylist service for television commercial films. From then on, there was no stopping her. She became an Art Director to both feature and commercial films, wrote a book for children, built up an amazing reference library, does endless voluntary hospital work and goodness knows what else. She is a friend who is always there in one's hour of need. Inevitably, she is an excellent cook.

## Maria's Gazpacho

MARIANNE FORD

Richard Ford, when he wrote the *Gatherings from Spain* in 1846, could not have imagined that it would instil in his descendants such an interest in gazpacho. Over the years we must have put every recipe to the test. Since 1960 it has been Maria's (Mama's old Andalusian cook) that has remained the staunch family favourite. A blunt, worn and battered *mouli* kept solely for this purpose is the proof of its popularity. Richard Ford writes, 'Any remarks on Spanish salads would be incomplete without some account of gazpacho, that vegetable soup, or floating salad . . . Reapers and agricultural labourers could never stand the sun's fire without this cooling acetous diet.'

Serves 6–8

3 slices bread

10 fl oz milk

2 lb tomatoes, scalded and peeled

1 cucumber, grated

1 large onion, grated

1 green pepper, grated

28 fl oz tomato juice

2 cloves garlic

about $\frac{1}{2}$ tsp coarse salt

2 tbsp oil

1 tbsp vinegar

pepper, to taste

dash of Tabasco, to taste

1. Cut the crust off the bread and chop into small breadcrumbs. Put them into a bowl and pour on the milk.
2. Put tomatoes, cucumber, onion and pepper through the *mouli*.
3. Using a pestle and mortar, pound the garlic into the coarse salt until it becomes a smooth paste.
4. Add the bread.
5. Stir well and add the tomato juice, oil, vinegar and pepper.
6. Mix well and, if necessary, add a little water to get a smooth consistency.
7. Put it and the soup plates into the refrigerator to cool.

# *Christmas*

*R.D.* I loathe Christmas.

Christmas is for children. Sixty-five and seventy years ago, when I was small, Christmas was entirely a family affair and very wonderful it was. The stocking was always hung at the end of the bed the night before and the next morning it would be filled with simple things, like an orange, some nuts, a tiny model Dinky car, a puzzle, some pencils and perhaps even a fountain pen. The main presents, never very expensive or elaborate, were wrapped up under the Christmas tree, and they were nearly all from the family. The toys were clock-work and we loved them. The Meccano sets were made of metal, not plastic. The jigsaw puzzles were cut from wood, not cardboard, the teddy bears were of wool, not poly-something-or-other, and the china dolls had eyes that shut when you laid them down. Nowadays all toys are battery-run, with remote-control gadgets and complex electronic mechanisms that go wrong after a week. Everything is expensive and full of silicon chips.

Christmas is also a time when a fair number of adults who never go to church during the rest of the year go to morning service to sing jolly songs and pay their annual dues to Christianity. But basically Christmas has become an obscene festival, a bonanza for shop-keepers, who get rich at the expense of the rest of the population, who get poor.

Present-giving among adults has reached a ridiculous level. Long lists are compiled, not just of relatives and close friends, but of all sorts of acquaintances who you don't really care very much about. You live in fear that someone you've left out will give you a present and it will be too late to give one back. Everything has to be tit for tat, that is the golden rule: 'I've got to get something for her because she always gives me one.'

The saddest thing about all this is that it puts a very serious financial strain on many young single working people, who find it hard enough to make ends meet anyway. Suddenly, once a year, convention compels them to fork out their savings. I hate it.

A few sensible folk make no-present agreements with each other, and to my mind everyone outside the immediate family and close friends should do this.

Christmas cards are another racket. I agree it is nice to send a once-a-year greeting to an old and distant friend. But apart from that, even longer lists are made out for Christmas cards than for presents. Everyone you can think of, including many people you've met only once in your life, gets one. And you yourself receive dozens of appalling cards from every business firm and trader you have ever dealt with. Your garage sends you one, so does your TV dealer and your fishmonger and anyone else who thinks you may spend money with him during the coming year. There is nothing more irritating than a Christmas card signed Anne, John or Jane. 'Why don't people put their surnames?' I invariably cry as the pile gets higher and higher.

Surely the worst racket of all is the charity Christmas card business. I know a bit about this because in 1989 Quentin Blake and I did a charity card. Had it not been for the help given to us by Penguin Books and others, very little money would have been raised. But Penguin persuaded the paper-makers, the envelope manufacturers, the printers and several other generous firms in the manufacturing chain to give everything free. Even then the cards wouldn't have sold if we had not allowed the booksellers to take their 30 or 40 per cent cut of the retail price. I am not telling you to ignore charity cards. They are better than non-charity ones. But you should be aware that, with the exception of a very few who make special arrangements, only a minute percentage of the price you pay finds its way to the charity itself. In many cases the people who make them and sell them to you take most of it.

Then you have the office parties, appalling drunken orgies at which the senior men, stupefied by drink and dribbling from the mouth, descend upon typists who they wouldn't deign to speak to during the rest of the year. The orgies are more common than you imagine and it's all part of the great Christian festival of Christmas.

And then comes the ritual of the turkey. It used always to be a goose (which tastes wonderful) or a plump capon, but some time ago someone decided that turkey was the thing to serve for Christmas dinner. Turkey breeders proliferated and millions of these birds were bred and fed in long sheds that kept their fluorescent lights on day and night to force the turkeys into gorging themselves round the clock. The breeders made a packet, as did the retailers, and soon virtually every family in Britain was stuffing itself at Christmas on one of the most tasteless meats that it is possible to find. I don't know quite what is drier and more flavourless than a roast turkey. Its only virtue seems to be that one bird goes a long way – so long, in fact, that the family is usually eating it cold or hashed up for the next week.

No, I don't like Christmas and always feel rather as though I have come through a long and fearful battle when it is over. Give it to the children by all means, but do not spoil them with over-expensive presents. Let all of us adults try to make it fun for the children, too, but heaven preserve us from trying to whip up false jollity among ourselves. Christmas used to be a wonderful and dignified Christian occasion. It is now the most important money-making period in the manufacturing industry.

A Christmas Feast

Almond Soup    Pike Quenelles

Stuffed Goose    Potato Cakes
Red & Green Cabbage    Brussel Sprouts    Sauce

Marwoods Mothers Mince Pies
Ginger Pudding    Christchurch Pudding

## Almond Soup

MARWOOD YEATMAN

This delicate soup, popular 100 years ago, is now unusual. On no account should it be liquidized at any stage, as that ruins the texture.

Serves 4–6

8 oz sweet almonds, blanched

3 hard-boiled egg yolks

2 pt strong chicken stock

*beurre manié*, made with 1 oz butter and 1 oz flour

5 fl oz single cream

salt and white pepper

1. Mince the almonds and, using a pestle and mortar, reduce to a paste with the egg yolks and a little stock, to stop them oiling.
2. Bring the stock up to simmering point in a saucepan and whisk in the *beurre manié*. When that has dissolved, whisk in the almond paste.
3. Cook gently for 30 minutes.
4. Strain through a sieve, add the cream, season with salt and pepper, heat gently and serve.

## Smoked Bacon and Split Yellow Pea Soup

SANDY

Serves 6

8 oz split yellow peas

6 rashers smoked streaky bacon

1 tbsp olive oil

2 carrots, neatly chopped

2 onions, neatly chopped

2 stalks celery, chopped

14-oz can tomatoes, drained and chopped

2 cloves garlic

1 bay leaf

6 stalks parsley

3 pt chicken stock

salt and black pepper

1. Place the dried peas in a bowl, cover with plenty of boiling water and soak for 1 hour. Drain before using.
2. Remove the rind and cut the bacon into strips.
3. Heat the olive oil in a saucepan and fry the bacon and the rind until lightly coloured.
4. Stir in the carrots, onions and celery and brown slightly.
5. Add the peas, tomatoes, garlic, bay leaf, parsley stalks and stock. Bring to the boil and simmer for 1 hour.
6. Remove bay leaf, bacon rind and parsley stalks, then season to taste with salt and pepper.

Serve with hot bread rolls.

# Michael

*R.D.* Michael is the husband of my youngest daughter, Lucy. He is also the son of the fabulous Cherokee Indian, Rose (p. 96), so Michael is himself one-half Cherokee. Michael and Lucy have a good marriage and two small children, and they live on a resort called Captiva Island on the Gulf side of the Florida peninsula. There they run a water-sport business, catering to the wealthy visitors by teaching them water-skiing, jet-boat riding, para-sailing and all the rest of it. Both of them are self-reliant, practical people who love the outdoor life they lead, and, naturally, they are both exceptional and original cooks. Here is Michael's recipe for chicken soup, which has become quite famous in our family. Apart from being very good, this soup is Michael's Marvellous Medicine and he insists on preparing it for Lucy whenever she is a little off-colour.

## Michael's Marvellous Medicine Chicken Soup

Serves 6

2 small or 1 large corn-fed chicken (total 5–6 lb)
4 small onions, peeled
4 oz mushrooms
3 large carrots
2 leeks
3 tsp chopped tarragon, preferably fresh
salt and pepper

1. Quarter the chicken, roughly chop 2 onions, place in a large saucepan and cover with water.

2. Bring to the boil and simmer until reduced by half. Top up and reduce by half again. This takes at least 4 hours. Cool.

3. Strain and reserve the liquid.

4. Pick the meat off the bones, chop and set aside. (If you have time, continue boiling the bones in fresh water, as in Step 2, to add more flavour to the stock.)

5. Chop remaining onions and other vegetables, add to the stock with the tarragon and cook until tender.

6. Season with salt and pepper to taste.

7. Before serving, add the meat and heat through.

# *Onions*

*R.D.* The vegetable that has always given me the greatest satisfaction to grow is the onion. I grow them large – the larger, the better – not only because a bed of huge onions is such a wonderful sight in August but also for their lovely mild-sweet taste, especially when eaten raw.

The finest large onions I have ever grown come from seed supplied by a small family nursery in the north, W. Robinson and Sons Ltd, Sunny Bank, Forton, near Preston, Lancashire PR3 0BN, and they are called Mammoth Improved Onion. My Robinson's onions weigh an average of 3 lb each, and because of their size they make marvellous, crisp, fried onion rings. Fried onion rings made from ordinary onions shrink to almost nothing when you fry them crisp, but not these. You can cook them in deep fat or in the pan, but make sure that you first dip them in seasoned flour. See recipe on p. 128.

# Josie's Smokies

If you are lucky enough to be near a good Italian shop, buy some olive oil bread to serve with these smokies.

You need 6 small ramekins.

Serves 6

10 oz smoked haddock
(or fish of your choice), skinned

3 tomatoes, skinned, seeded and neatly chopped

juice of $\frac{1}{2}$ lemon

3 tsp freshly chopped parsley

1 egg, lightly beaten

12 fl oz double cream

$1\frac{1}{2}$ oz grated Parmesan cheese *or* 3 oz fresh breadcrumbs fried in garlic butter

salt and pepper

chopped parsley

1. Preheat oven to 375°F / 190°C / Gas mark 5.
2. Place equal quantities of sliced fish and tomato in each ramekin.
3. Sprinkle with the lemon juice and chopped parsley.
4. Combine the lightly beaten egg with the cream and season well.
5. Pour the cream mixture over the fish.
6. Sprinkle with Parmesan cheese or garlic breadcrumbs.
7. Bake in oven for 15–20 minutes, until lightly golden and bubbling.
8. Sprinkle with chopped parsley and serve.

# Onion Soup

CALLIE

Serves 6

3 oz butter

6 large onions, sliced

2 cloves garlic, sliced

2 heaped tsp Dijon mustard

1 heaped tsp Marmite extract

3 pt very good chicken stock

1 bay leaf

salt and pepper

GARNISH

8 oz grated Gruyère cheese

1 baguette loaf sliced in $\frac{1}{2}$-in.-thick *croûtes*

1. Melt the butter in a large saucepan. Soften and brown the onion and garlic very slowly for over 2 hours. This is the *essence* of a successful onion soup.
2. Add the mustard, Marmite, stock and bay leaf and bring to the boil.
3. Reduce to the desired consistency. This could vary from a consommé-type soup to one that is much thicker.
4. Taste and correct seasoning.
5. Toast the *croûtes* and top each with some grated Gruyère. Place under a grill until melted and lightly browned.

Serve the soup and place the *croûtes* on the top.

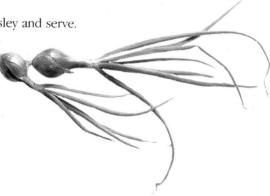

*Onion soup*

## Spiv's Soft Herring Roe Soufflé

### ANN TWICKEL

Liccy is my niece. Her mother and I were brought up in the family home of the Throckmortons, Coughton Court in Warwickshire. The kitchens at Coughton were very large and situated to cause the maximum inconvenience to everyone concerned. The house was built on three sides of a square, with the kitchens at the very end of the north side and the dining-room on the first floor of the south. This entailed all the food being carried either through the whole house or, in fine weather, by a short cut across the courtyard. Nevertheless, I have no recollection of a tepid dish or a collapsed soufflé arriving on the table. Family legend, however, claimed that the latter disaster did once occur and during the subsequent panic a flushed and out-of-breath bootboy rushed up to the cook with the offer of his bicycle pump.

This recipe is from Liccy's younger sister, Spiv. It doesn't use flour, as the roes give the soufflé a good consistency.

Serves 4–5

butter and grated Parmesan cheese
for greasing and lining the 7-in. soufflé dish

1 lb soft herring roes

2 oz butter

1 tsp salt

fresh ground black pepper

1 oz grated Gruyère cheese

4 egg yolks

6 egg whites

1 oz grated Parmesan cheese

1. Preheat oven to 450°F / 230°C / Gas mark 8.
2. Generously butter a 7-in. soufflé dish and sprinkle sides with a little Parmesan to aid the rising. Place upside-down in the freezer until needed.
3. Pick the black stringy bits off the roes. Fry gently in butter. Purée the mixture in a food processor, but do not liquidize. Add salt and pepper and Gruyère.
4. Beat egg yolks.
5. Whisk egg whites to peaks.
6. Gently add roe mixture to yolks and then gradually fold in the whites using a metal spatula. Pour into soufflé dish. Sprinkle remaining Parmesan on top.
7. Place in the oven for exactly 17 minutes. Don't peep – it always works and is crisp on top and gooey in the middle.

Eat as a savoury, with water to drink, as wine is ruined by roes!

## Herring Terrine

### JOSIE

This is an excellent first course for a dinner party. It is best made the day before, as this gives it a chance to set well, making the slicing easier.
You will need a 3-pt terrine.

Serves 12

prosciutto ham *or* blanched whole spinach
leaves, stalks removed, to line the terrine

1–2 oz clarified butter

black pepper and grated nutmeg, to taste

5 whole kippers

$3\frac{1}{2}$ baking potatoes

8-oz slab of bacon cut into $2\frac{1}{2}$-in. cubes

3 small onions, sliced

1 fl oz whisky

1 egg, beaten

salt, to taste

1. Line the terrine with kitchen foil, leaving enough hanging over the edges to fold over and cover the top later.

2. Now line the terrine with either the ham or blanched spinach leaves, leaving no gaps and allowing enough ham or spinach overhanging to fold over and cover the top later. Use the clarified butter to stick the ham or spinach together at the joins.

3. Season the sides and base with some of the pepper and nutmeg.

4. Scrub the potatoes and place in the pre-heated oven at 400°F / 200°C / Gas mark 6 for 30 minutes, until half-baked.

5. Bake the kippers at the same temperature for about 5 minutes to make boning easier. Bone and skin the fish.

6. Set oven to 350°F / 180°C / Gas mark 4.

7. Sweat the bacon and onion together in a pan over low heat until soft.

8. Scoop the potatoes out of their skins and mash.

9. Mince the bacon and onions, and place in a mixing bowl.

10. Add the fish to the bacon and onion paste.

11. Mix thoroughly, adding the mashed potato.

12. Add the whisky and egg, and season well with salt, pepper and nutmeg.

13. Place mixture in the lined terrine, and gently bang the terrine to remove any air pockets.

14. Fold over the ham or spinach to cover the mixture, then fold over the foil to cover the top.

15. Place the lid on the terrine and stand terrine on some paper in a *bain marie* and bake for about 50 minutes. To test, place a skewer in the centre of the terrine for about 1 minute. If the skewer is clean and warm when removed, then the terrine is cooked. It will also feel firm when pressed.

Serve with plenty of Melba toast, but no butter.

Because this is a finely ground terrine, it should be thinly sliced with a knife blade that has been dipped in hot water before each slice; this prevents the terrine sticking to the blade.

## Scandinavian Herrings

PIP

Serves 4

12 matjes herring fillets, sliced into large pieces
4 fl oz mayonnaise
1 tbsp medium curry powder
4 fl oz sour cream
1 sharp dessert apple, finely chopped
1 small leek, finely chopped
1 tbsp sugar
salt and black pepper, to taste

1. Mix curry powder into the mayonnaise.
2. Place the reddish, sweet, spicy herrings in the mayonnaise and sour cream.
3. Add the chopped apple, chopped leek, sugar and salt and pepper.
4. Marinate overnight and check the sugar and seasoning; adjust if necessary.

Serve with sliced buttered rye bread.

# Kaa Indana Kiazi

*R.D.* Way back in 1938 when I was working in Dar es Salaam for the Shell Company, three of us Shell boys shared a large house outside the town high up on the cliffs above the Indian Ocean. I was in charge of the catering for our household and every morning I held a solemn conference about the supper menu with our cook, a wizened old charmer from the Mwanumwezi tribe who was affectionately known as Piggy. We ate mostly the delicious fish caught in the sea just below us by another old man, called Mvuvi, who fished from a dugout canoe. Mvuvi was also a great catcher of crabs, and from these huge spidery creatures Piggy the Cook used to make a dish so simple and yet so glorious that we had it twice every week for our evening meal. The dish was called Kaa Indana Kiazi, which means simply Crab in Potato, and this is how Piggy made it.

He took one large potato per person and put them in the oven to bake. While they were baking he cooked the crabs and extracted from them only the white meat, but lots of it. He made a small quantity of béchamel sauce and mixed the crab meat into it. When the potatoes were baked, he opened them up on top and scooped out most but not quite all of their insides. He then filled the potatoes with the crab meat mixture and put them back in the oven and baked them some more until the skins were very crisp. They were served hot and devoured with gusto.

## *Piggy's Potatoes*

*L.D.* Piggy's recipe is glorious but, using English crabs and a little improvisation, we have managed one almost as good.

Serves 4

2 large baking potatoes

salt and pepper

knob of butter

milk

3 tbsp fish velouté, made from 1 oz butter, 1 oz flour and 10 fl oz fish stock (roux method)

1 large crab (ask fishmonger to remove the dead-man's fingers for you), from which you will need 5 heaped tbsp white crab meat and 2 heaped tbsp dark crab meat

2 heaped tsp sour cream

juice of $\frac{1}{2}$ lemon

a small bunch of fresh parsley or dill, chopped

1. Preheat oven to 450°F / 230°C / Gas mark 8.

2. Scrub potato skins clean, prick with fork, wet or butter them and sprinkle with salt. Bake for about 1 hour.

3. Cut the potatoes in half. Scoop out the potato, leaving about $\frac{1}{4}$-in. lining. (For an even crispier potato case, deep-fry in a mixture of half corn oil, half olive oil.)

4. Mash the potato with salt, pepper, butter and a little milk.

5. Add the fish velouté and the sour cream together.

6. Mix in the dark crab meat, lemon juice and dill.

7. Gently fold in the white crab meat.

8. Fill potato cases with the mixture and bake in the oven for 5 minutes, until heated through and golden on top.

9. Sprinkle with chopped parsley or dill.

# La Rochelle

*R.D.*   There was a dinner Liccy and I had in La Rochelle. I have close relations in this lovely town. My father's Norwegian brother, Uncle Oscar, went there years ago to make his fortune and did so by building up a fleet of fishing trawlers called 'Pêcheurs d'Atlantique'. Uncle Oscar died nearly seventy years ago but his son, my cousin Eric, took over. Eric is now also dead, but seven years ago when Liccy and I drove down to see him he was still very much alive. He lived in a fine, old stone house in the very centre of La Rochelle and I am not exaggerating when I say that the interior was like a museum dedicated to beauty. Louis XIV sofas and chairs with their original needle-work covering, paintings by Greuze and Loussain and Boucher, Savonnerie carpets, shelves full of rare books and perhaps the finest collection of sea shells in the world.

Eric took the two of us out to dinner in a La Rochelle restaurant and said, 'Here you will taste the finest fish there is.' The day before, he had ordered marinated raw sardines (the real French ones, about six inches long) and had carefully arranged that when they arrived at the restaurant they had been no more than half an hour out of the sea. The chef had then placed them in a marinade for twenty-four hours. What was the marinade composed of, we asked. 'Ah', came the reply, 'I never divulge my secrets.' However we squeezed out of him the fact that it was mainly fine olive oil and herbs. That is all he would tell us.

Never had either of us tasted fish like that. We went mad about it and Cousin Eric smiled and nodded and said, 'All fish, even more so than vegetables, have to be very, very fresh. Every minute counts.' The fish itself had been cut up into more or less square pieces and it was so tender and so incredibly tasty that we couldn't get over it. I am at a loss to describe it better. Liccy and I went back to the restaurant the next morning and ordered some more for our picnic lunch but, alas, they were totally inferior. They had been caught the day before. So I suppose the lesson we learn from this is that if you ever catch a fish yourself, cook it at once. Don't wait.

*Algarvian style clams*

## Mussels or Clams Algarvian Style

### RUTH

Serves 4 as a first course or 2 as a main course

2¼ lb mussels *or* cherry-stone clams

9 fl oz oil: half good-quality olive oil,
half good-quality corn oil

1 bunch fresh coriander leaves, roughly
chopped

6 cloves garlic, roughly chopped

17 fl oz white wine

juice of ½ lemon

salt and pepper, to taste

1. Wash clams or mussels well in cold running water.
2. Heat oil in a large wide saucepan.
3. Add roughly chopped garlic and coriander to the oil.
4. Cook for a couple of minutes, then add mussels or clams, white wine and lemon juice, salt and pepper.
5. Place lid on saucepan, cook and shake pan a couple of times.
6. When mussels or clams are open, pour into soup plates with plenty of the liquid.

Serve immediately with lemon wedges and plenty of crusty bread to mop up the juice.

## Scallop and Spinach Dainties

### FRANÇOIS CLERC

Ideal for what we call posh dinners. It looks very impressive and is delicious. You will need 6 ramekins.

Serves 6

2 large onions

1 oz clarified butter

8 oz fresh spinach, cleaned

salt, pepper and grated nutmeg, to taste

16 large scallops

2 tomatoes

5 tbsp double cream

1 tbsp lemon juice

#### GARNISH

tomato *bâtons* (fine strips) and chervil

1. Thinly slice the onions. Place them in a saucepan with the butter and cook very slowly for 2 hours. Towards the end add the spinach and cook until tender.
2. Roughly chop the spinach mixture and season well with salt, pepper and nutmeg.
3. Thinly slice the scallops and lay them in the bottom of the ramekins.
4. Divide the spinach mixture equally and place on top of the scallops.
5. Preheat oven to 400°F / 200°C / Gas mark 6.
6. To prepare the sauce, peel, seed and purée the tomatoes.
7. Add cream and lemon juice to the purée, and season.
8. Place the ramekins in the oven for 5 minutes.

To serve, turn out the scallops on to the centre of a plate, spoon some of the sauce around and garnish.

*Moules à l'escargot*

## Moules à l'Escargot

### JANE GRIGSON

*L.D.* Having always loved this recipe, I asked Eleo, my editor, who had known and worked with Jane Grigson, to write to her for permission to use it. Her reply is opposite. I was so touched by this letter, sent only a couple of days before she died, that I have asked her daughter's permission to publish it to show Jane Grigson's immense generosity.

This is an inexpensive dish. A bag of *moules* will easily feed six people, allowing a dozen mussels each.

FOR THE MUSSELS

5 fl oz white wine

a few stalks of parsley

1 large cob loaf, granary or wholemeal

*ESCARGOT* BUTTER
(*covers approximately 75 mussels*)

12 oz unsalted butter

2 oz chopped parsley

$1\frac{1}{2}$ oz finely chopped shallots

4 cloves garlic, crushed

freshly ground black pepper

sea salt

a little lemon juice

1. Wash, scrub, debeard and remove any barnacles from the mussels.
2. Discard any that are broken (damaged or will not close when tapped).

3. Put the mussels in a large saucepan with wine and parsley stalks and cover with a lid.
4. Place over moderately hot heat for approximately 5 minutes, shaking the pan rigorously a couple of times, until the mussels have opened.
5. Drain them in a colander and cool.
6. Preheat oven to 400°F / 200°C / Gas mark 6.
7. Mix all the ingredients for the butter together until evenly mixed.
8. Split the shells apart so you have a mussel in each, discard the remaining shells. Fill shell by covering each with the butter, using a knife to spread it on.
9. Slice the loaf of bread horizontally into $\frac{1}{4}$-in.-thick round slices.
10. With an apple corer, make holes in the slices where you will place the mussels, trying to get 12 on each, if possible. Otherwise, you will need 2 slices of bread with 6 mussels on each for one portion.
11. Place the bread on a baking tray with mussels resting on the holes.
12. Place in the oven for 7–10 minutes until the butter has melted and is bubbling.

Serve immediately. The toast will have soaked up the garlic juice and will be delicious to eat.

As an alternative, try the mussels with this mushroom butter.

MUSHROOM BUTTER

12 oz unsalted butter

3 oz chopped parsley

2 oz chopped mushrooms

2 slices cooked ham

5 cloves garlic, crushed

salt and pepper

Mix all ingredients together and spread over the mussels in their shells as before, and cook as above.

March 3rd, 1990

Dear Eleo,

    Yes, of course.  I really do not mind if anyone uses any
of my recipes, so long as there's an acknowledgement.

    In fact surely anyone can use anyone's recipe, so long as
they rewrite it, with or without acknowledgement?  I rather
deplore the habit that has grown up of having to write round to
ask permission - it adds to the labour of the book and fulfils no
legal obligation. In fact the person quoted ought to be grateful
for the free publicity, and humbly recollect the number of times
they have pilfered from fellow writers past and present. In cooking
originality is rare, it's all a matter of adjustment and balance
and I certainly did not invent moules farcies. I suppose the honour
ought to go to Melanie, that Breton cook discovered by Curnonsky,
and her praires farcies which has become a standard dish of
French cookery outside Brittany as well, and which has been
adapted to mussels/oysters/other clams.

    I am bashing away at <u>English Food</u>, and think that re-publication
may fall well with this new turn towards <u>cuisine grande-mère</u>. At the
moment things are not to bad on the cancer-front, let's hope I can
hold up for a few months longer, perhaps even a year or two.

    Incidentally the mussel piece you sent me was published in
the Observer magazine. One editor (among the many I've managed to
survive) had a passion for short weekly pieces, right against the
usually more discursive style and length.

Best wishes

Yours

Jane

## Smoked Salmon Strudel

### JOSIE

The strudel can be served either as a first course or as a light lunch.

Makes 4 individual strudels

2 eggs

3 oz smoked salmon, slices or pieces

10 fl oz double cream

2 oz butter

1 tsp flour

2 tsp chopped chives or thinly sliced spring onions

salt

juice and zest of 1 lemon

4 leaves filo pastry

1. Hard-boil eggs. When cold, peel and chop finely, and place in a bowl.

2. Dice the smoked salmon and add to the eggs.

3. Pour the cream into a saucepan and bring to the boil.

4. In a separate bowl mix 1 tsp butter to a paste with the flour and whisk this into the cream until the mixture thickens.

5. Stir in the eggs and salmon, chives or spring onions, and add the lemon zest and juice. Season to taste and allow to cool.

6. Preheat oven to 400°F / 200°C / Gas mark 6.

7. Melt the remaining butter.

8. Lay a sheet of filo pastry on a clean, dry, flat surface and brush it with some of the butter.

9. Fold in half to create a double layer. Repeat this with the remaining 3 sheets of pastry.

10. Place equal quantities of the salmon mixture on the end of each sheet, fold in the sides and roll up.

11. Bake in the oven for about 15 minutes, until crisp and golden.

Serve immediately with a watercress salad tossed in dressing, and with garlic *croûtons*.

## Tartare of Salmon and Smoked Haddock

### PIP

A wonderful summer recipe.
Marinating time: 4–5 hours for fish, 2 hours for cucumber.

Serves 4

2–3 tbsp fresh chopped dill

5 fl oz sour cream

juice of $\frac{1}{2}$ lemon

salt and pepper

6 oz fresh salmon, cut into small cubes

6 oz smoked haddock, cut into small cubes

4 tsp white wine vinegar

2 tsp sugar

1 cucumber, peeled and very thinly sliced

GARNISH

sprigs of fresh dill

1. Mix together the chopped dill, sour cream, lemon juice, and salt and pepper to taste.

2. Place the cubes of fish on a large, flat dish and cover with the marinade. Leave for 4–5 hours.

3. Meanwhile, mix together the vinegar, sugar, a generous sprinkling of salt, and pepper to taste, and marinate the cucumber in this mixture for 2 hours.

4. Drain the excess marinade off the fish, although most of it will be coating the fish.

5. Fill a small ramekin with quarter of the fish mixture and turn out on to an individual plate. Repeat this with the remaining fish.

6. Drain the cucumber and arrange in an overlapping layer around the fish.

Garnish and serve with hot bread.

# Pike Quenelles

## MARWOOD YEATMAN

On summer mornings, the rods often wait outside Bob the Fish for him to open the shop and buy the salmon they killed in the pool below the bridge in town, or down river by the weir. This time, when I passed at eight o'clock, there was a boy standing in the doorway holding a pike. Its tail was touching the ground and the head came up to the middle of his chest.

A few minutes later, I joined Bob and the boy in the back of the shop. The pike was lying on the floor. It was as deep as a salmon, over a yard long, and the huge, distended mouth, slightly open, was inches wide. I could see the teeth.

'Some fish, isn't she?' Bob said. 'I'm glad I didn't have to carry her home.'

The boy smiled proudly. I inspected the pike. She was three times the size of the one that had recently slipped past me in the shallows by the mill while I was looking for crayfish, but every bit as sleek and firm.

'Did she fight?' I asked the boy.

'She ran like hell.'

The sun shone through the window on the pike, lighting up her brilliant eyes and skin. She was in the most beautiful and lustrous condition, silver underneath, streamlined in gold, and a deep, dark green along her back, the colour of the reeds in the river.

'Do you want her?' I asked Bob.

'I don't mind.'

I turned to the boy. 'How much?'

'Tenner.'

I was not going to argue, and paid him. He pocketed the money, thanked us both and left. Bob picked up the fish by the eyes, the easiest way to hold a pike, and with some effort hooked it on to the scales. We studied the weight.

'Having a party?' he said.

'No.'

'Anyone else?'

'Not at the moment.'

'What the devil are you going to do with 28 lb of pike, then?'

I felt the broad shoulders of the fish, and ran my hand down the body, over the fin, to the wide sweep of the cool and powerful tail. 'I don't know, yet,' I said. 'I just had to buy it.'

The pike is a luminous shadow amongst other fish till he feels hungry, and they, sensing danger, keep away. Then he moves to the cover of a tributary or reed bed, and waits. He is stealthy, unin- hibited, swift and savage, striking with a violent flourish and leaving the river ominously still. A pike is more than a shark. He is death. He will attack salmon, trout and cyprinoids his own size and larger, swallowing them in stages, frogs, birds, and close relations too. It is not unusual to find pike inside pike inside pike or see baby wild duck, out for a swim behind their mother, disappear from the surface of a lake with a sinister plop. Nothing can be so destructive in fresh water, reach a larger size and perform genuine feats more often exaggerated by man, but never, quite, to be discounted. One look into the dark rhines and forbidding pools of the west and fens by Whittlesey Mere is enough to provoke an image of rogue pike, monster pike, taking swans in flight, seizing mules and milkmaids, and drowning Alsatian dogs. Only perch and tench are known to be safe. For other victims, once bitten, to struggle is useless. There is no escape from that terrible mouth, encrusted with teeth, all pointing inwards. You can see them on the heads, dried up and grinning, nailed to keepers' huts like stoats on a gibbet.

Pike are in season from July until March. If ever they appear in the shops, it is usually in the autumn and early winter, convenient for Christmas, when the trout streams are electro-fished for predators. A pike thus taken may have a broken back from the charge. Cut around the bruise. Their roe is emetic, possibly poisonous.

The high prices fetched by pike in medieval England are hard to understand today. Even the fittest-looking specimen, well larded, is apt to taste and smell muddy. Very little can be done with a large fish except cold-smoke it. A jack or a side of less than 4 lb or so should be made into quenelles, the fluffy dumplings of the Edwardian dining table. For these, the meat is equal or superior to salmon, veal or chicken. It has the perfect gelatinous consistency and somehow acquires a pleasant taste through the other ingredients.

Quenelles are not seen much in private houses now. They are for serious cooks and fiddly to prepare, but nothing so sophisticated is easier to serve or more economical. A 4-lb pike, which may be given away by a water bailiff, makes a couple of dozen dumplings. The only expense is the labour.

## Pike Quenelles

1 lb fish makes 14–16 quenelles

First, fillet and skin a pike. Remove the awkward right-angle bones with pliers. Pulp the meat in a mincer or *mouli*. Weigh it. For every 1 lb of fish, proceed as follows.

### CHOUX PASTE

2 oz butter

10 fl oz water

4 oz flour

2 eggs

### FISH SEASONING

5 fl oz single cream

$\frac{1}{2}$ level tsp salt

$\frac{1}{4}$ level tsp white pepper

### SAUCE

$\frac{1}{2}$ oz butter

1 small onion

1 glass dry white wine

$1\frac{1}{2}$ pt béchamel, made with $1\frac{1}{2}$ oz butter, $1\frac{1}{2}$ oz flour and $1\frac{1}{2}$ pt milk

2–4 oz grated or crumbled mature Cheshire or Lancashire cheese

5 fl oz single cream

salt and pepper to taste

1. To make the choux paste, put the butter in a pan with the water and boil.

2. When the butter is melted, remove from the heat and add the flour all at once. Stir vigorously to get rid of any lumps.

3. Cook gently, still stirring, until the paste leaves the sides of the pan. Remove from the heat, cover and allow to cool slightly.

4. Mix in the eggs.

5. Mix the fish seasoning ingredients into the pike, then mix in the paste. Push the lot through a sieve with a ladle or plastic scraper. Chill (a cold preparation is easier to handle).

6. To cook the quenelles, collect 2 pans of hot water. Bring one up to simmering point over a moderate heat. Wet your hands in the other to stop the dumplings sticking to your skin. Roll up a quantity of the chilled mixture about the size of a hen's egg, smoothing over any cracks. Drop immediately into the pan of simmering water. Repeat the process, washing your hands in the other pan of water each time. The quenelles will sink at first, but soon rise to the surface.

7. Poach for 15–20 minutes in total. Prod gently: when the dumplings are beginning to feel solid, and look swollen, they are done. Remove with a perforated spoon, and drain. Set aside until required. Always allow the quenelles to cool to room temperature before chilling or freezing.

   The raw quenelle mixture can also be baked. Use either buttered individual moulds or a terrine standing in a pan of hot water and place in the oven at 300°F / 150°C / Gas mark 2. The preparation will take about 50–75 minutes to cook, depending on the size of the container. It is done when shrunken from the sides, and should turn out easily. Cut the terrine into slices and serve with the sauce.

8. To make the sauce, melt the butter in a pan, add the onion and sweat until soft.

9. Deglaze with the wine and reduce by half.

10. Lower the heat and mix in the béchamel.

11. Add cheese; cook gently until melted.

12. Enrich with the cream and adjust seasoning.

13. To serve the quenelles, put them in a greased baking dish and cover with buttered greaseproof paper. Heat through in the oven for about 1 hour at 300°F / 150°C / Gas mark 2. Pour the hot sauce over the quenelles and send them to the table.

*Pike quenelles*

# Betty d'Abreu

## SPIV BARRAN

My and Liccy's mother was born in 1906 as Elizabeth Throckmorton. She came from a grand old Catholic recusant family, traceable back to pre-Domesday times. An earlier Elizabeth Throckmorton had displeased Queen Elizabeth I by marrying Sir Walter Raleigh. 'Betty' was used to meals produced in the traditional upper-class manner, by a cook and kitchen maids, and with butler and housemaid to wait at table. She would rarely have ventured into the kitchen to cook, but she had a fine appreciation of good food.

However, as a young woman my mother broke ranks by becoming a nurse at St Thomas's hospital. She was someone who, like her daughter Liccy Dahl, couldn't stand by and watch others less fortunate than herself suffer. She had to help, quietly and effectively.

It was at St Thomas's that she first encountered cookery, in the dietitian's kitchen. She used one of her other great talents, her artistic ability, to illustrate a magazine serial written by a fellow nurse.

As a nurse she met my father, Pon d'Abreu, a fantastically handsome young doctor, and married him despite family disapprobation. At first she had to mastermind very frugal meals, as money was tight, and then cope with wartime shortages and rationing. Later, she entertained family and friends and, on a more lavish scale, visiting doctors, often from far-off countries. By then my father had become Professor of Surgery at Birmingham University.

My mother always kept her own cookery books, with neatly written recipes from the Throckmorton kitchens at Coughton, and others culled from newspapers, magazines or friends, or from her own imagination. She always took immense care with the presentation of the food. Her artistic pride meant that no one else in the family was ever allowed to lay the table for Christmas dinner!

My father was a fussy eater. He couldn't stand to eat cold meals, so they were reserved for weekday lunchtimes: his loss, for her salads were superb. My mother managed to satisfy my father's tastes in food and yet bring a touch of flair and originality to meals (as the following recipe shows). There was always a great sense of balance, which perhaps stemmed from her dietitian's training.

She drank very little and was once caught pouring her sherry into a pot plant at some official medical reception! But she adored champagne and sloe gin (not together!), which she would make herself in the autumn and savour in minute thimblefuls at Christmas.

A bon viveur on a modest scale, with a well-rounded figure, given to occasional hopeless attempts at 'banting' (her word), my mother was happiest sitting at the head of the family dining-room table enjoying a good meal. All her three daughters are just the same.

## Betty d'Abreu's Pea Dish

*L.D.* Upon the arrival of the first summer peas the family was gathered into the garden to pick and pod for this delicate and delicious dish, which we always ate as a first course as it is too rich to accompany another dish. Only the smallest peas were used, the larger ones separated to have as an accompanying vegetable to the main course the next day. It became a summer ritual.

Really fresh peas make this dish special, but top-quality frozen *petits pois* can be used.

Serves 6

6 spring onions
1 lb shelled peas
1 tsp sugar
2 oz prosciutto ham
5 fl oz single cream
salt
black pepper
¼ tsp grated nutmeg

1. Chop onions into 1-in. pieces and boil with peas in water with sugar for about 3 minutes.

2. Cut prosciutto into 1-in. strips (sharp scissors are best).

3. Heat cream with salt, pepper and nutmeg to just below boiling point and combine with drained peas, onions and prosciutto.

4. Bake at 350°F / 180°C / Gas mark 4 for 15 minutes and serve.

## Stilton Pâté

ANNE

This is excellent either as a first course or eaten with what remains of the wine after the main course. It needs about 2 hours' chilling time before serving.

Serves 6

8 oz full-fat soft cheese

2 tbsp dry white wine

2 tbsp single cream

6 oz Stilton cheese, rind removed, finely grated

1 oz finely sliced celery

1 tsp finely chopped shallot

1 tbsp chopped parsley

freshly grated nutmeg

salt and pepper

1. In a food processor beat the soft cheese with the wine and cream to a smooth, creamy mixture.
2. Add the Stilton cheese, celery, shallot and parsley, and season to taste with the nutmeg, salt and pepper.
3. Form the mixture into a tight, neat roll about $1\frac{1}{2}$ in. thick. Wrap in cling film, secure ends and refrigerate for about 2 hours.

Cut the pâté into slices and serve with toast.

## Tomato Jelly Ring

ARABELLA BOXER

Adapted from a recipe by Arabella Boxer, this makes an ideal buffet dish. It would be best to prepare it in a 3-pt ring mould.

Serves 10–12

$2 \times 14$-oz cans peeled tomatoes

1 pt chicken stock

6 slices onion

2 stalks celery or $\frac{1}{2}$ tsp celery salt

4 stalks parsley

2 bay leaves

10 peppercorns

1 tsp sugar

a generous pinch of cayenne pepper

salt and black pepper

1 oz gelatin

1. Put all the ingredients except the gelatin in a pan and bring slowly to the boil. Cover and simmer gently for 20 minutes.
2. Remove bay leaves, liquidize and pass through a sieve. There should be $1\frac{1}{2}$–2 pt. Season well.
3. Dissolve gelatin in enough warm water to make the sieved liquid up to 2 pt and strain into it. Mix well.
4. Pour into a ring mould and chill.

To serve, dip the mould into hot water for a few seconds and then turn out on to a plate and fill the centre with: chopped hard-boiled eggs mixed with a little cream and 1 tbsp finely chopped chives *or* diced cucumber and prawn, mixed with $2\frac{1}{2}$ fl oz cream or yoghurt, 2 tsp olive oil, 1 tsp lemon juice, salt, pepper and cayenne.

*Tomato jelly ring*

# Town Farm

*May and Alan Bedford*

*R.D.* In our village, right off the High Street, there is a farm that transports you straight into the sixteenth century the moment you walk into the yard. Calves are born and reared in the old cowsheds, hens and ducks and bantams wander all over the place, ferrets stare at you with pork eyes from their wooden cages, innumerable cats and kittens prowl around the hayricks, and in the lambing season there are usually two or three orphaned lambs wandering about and being fed by hand.

The huge old barn is a wonder to behold, but the massive timbers are usually hidden by the bales of hay that are stacked up to the roof. Rusty old ploughs and other derelict machinery lie around in the sheds tangled up with broken wagon-wheels and extraordinary implements made of iron in a bygone age.

Out of the tangled undergrowth and nettles behind the barns and sheds everything seems to grow better for Alan Bedford than for anyone else. His cherries are huge and black. His redcurrants are the size of grapes and his pears are sweet and juicy. But most of all, the eggs that are laid by his wandering hens are the best you can get. In our house we eat no others. We are lucky to get them. They come to us in return for the grazing-rights in our orchard that we give to Alan for his young cattle.

One of the most satisfying suppers in the world is composed simply of two fried eggs from Alan Bedford's hens and three huge rashers of bacon from Richard Woodall in Cumberland. The Woodalls have run a ham and bacon business in the tiny village of Waberthwaite for seven generations. They will sell you their own Parma-style ham (possibly better and certainly less expensive than the Italian variety and air-dried in exactly the same way) either on or off the bone, their own Cumberland ham, raw or cooked, and, of course, their own home-cured bacon, sold by the flitch, which is a 2-foot long column as thick as your arm.

# Oeufs en Gelée

*R.D.* To me this is the most beautiful and delicious dish, but it is difficult to make well. If you can succeed in having the eggs not only soft-boiled inside but also separately suspended in the jelly, and yet not having the jelly too firm, then you have achieved the miracle.

## Oeufs en Gelée

### JOSIE

The quantities for this dish depend upon the number of people and the size and shape of the serving bowl. It's well worth practising this before serving it for the first time – allow plenty of time and patience! (Of course, the dish will taste just as good and be simpler to prepare if you make each serving in an individual ramekin.)

Approximately 10 eggs

2 pt good quality chicken consommé

4 pt water

$1\frac{3}{4}$ oz aspic

1 bunch fresh tarragon, chopped

1. Place eggs in boiling water for $3\frac{1}{2}$–4 minutes. Run under cold water and allow to cool. Peel very carefully.
2. Put the chicken consommé and water in a saucepan and bring to the boil.
3. Dissolve the aspic in the consommé and allow to cool.
4. Make sure the serving bowl is clean.
5. Set a separate bowl over ice. Place some aspic in it, add a little chopped tarragon and stir occasionally until it is at the point of setting.
6. Pour into the serving bowl and allow to set.
7. Place an egg or two on top of the set aspic.
8. Pour some more aspic into the bowl set over ice, add a little chopped tarragon and stir occasionally until it is at the point of setting.
9. Now quickly and carefully pour this over the eggs resting on the set aspic.

   Judgement is needed to guess the correct amount of aspic to cover the eggs. Also great care is needed when the aspic is about to set to get the tarragon suspended and not floating on the top, causing lines when the dish is completed.
10. Repeat until all the eggs are used. Allow time for the last eggs to set in the aspic.

Place the bowl on the table and allow each guest to spoon out his or her egg! Serve with toast.

## Callie's Quiche

*L.D.* This fine dish demonstrates that some good can come out of misfortune. Callie had a French boyfriend, who was known to all of us in the family as The Frog. The Frog lived with his mother somewhere in France, and like lots of other mothers, especially the French ones, La Mère Frog was a superb cook. Her *pièce de résistance* was her quiche. Callie rather cleverly asked if she might be favoured with a lesson in quiche-making. La Mère Frog would normally never have agreed to divulge this great secret to a foreign girl, but this one was in love with her treasured son and vice versa, so the old lady consented and initiated Callie into the mysteries of quiche-making. Callie, being already an expert cook, didn't miss a trick, and when she came to us, she bowled us all over with this marvellous dish. The romance, alas, waned and withered but the quiche lived on.

*Callie's quiche*

My eldest daughter, Neisha, also had a brief love-affair with a French boy, and she saw quite a lot of his mother, but she squeezed no secrets out of her. Neisha was probably too scrupulous. But a keen cook should have no scruples at all when it comes to stealing from another cook. You may kiss the boyfriend goodbye, but always hang on to the recipe.

## Callie's Quiche

Serves 8

PÂTE A PÂTE

10 oz plain flour

½ tsp salt

7 oz margarine

2 egg yolks

up to 3 tbsp water

FILLING

3 oz butter

1 large onion, chopped

3 oz flour

about 1 pt milk

4 oz grated cheese, any variety

Dijon mustard, to taste

cayenne pepper, to taste

salt and pepper, to taste

about 8 oz streaky bacon, grilled to crispness and broken or cut into pieces

6 eggs, separated

1. To make the pastry, sieve the flour and salt into the food-processor bowl. Cut the margarine into small cubes and add to the flour. Using the pastry blade, whizz the mixture until it resembles fine breadcrumbs.

2. While it's still whizzing, add the 2 egg yolks with just enough water to combine the dough.

3. Lightly knead the dough into a ball. Wrap in cling film and place in the refrigerator to rest for at least 30 minutes.

4. Preheat oven to 400°F / 200°C / Gas mark 6.

5. Grease an 11-in. flan dish and roll out pastry thinly. Line the dish with the pastry, removing any air pockets.

6. Prick the base with a fork and bake blind for 20 minutes.

7. Having removed flan, turn oven up to 425–450°F / 220–230°C / Gas mark 7–8.

8. To make the filling, melt the butter, add the onion and cook until soft, then add the flour to make a roux.

9. Add milk, stirring slowly all the time until the sauce thickens to leave the sides of the pan.

10. Add the other ingredients except the egg whites.

11. Whisk the egg whites until stiff and fold into the filling mixture.

12. Pour the filling into the baked pastry case and bake for a further 30+ minutes at 425–450°F / 220–230°C / Gas mark 7–8.

Serve immediately to retain the soufflé effect. A green salad makes the perfect accompaniment.

# MAIN COURSES

Roast Partridges with Juniper Stuffing *60*

Casseroled Ptarmigan *61*

Jugged Hare *61*

Thai Chicken *62*

Chicken and Yoghurt Cream Curry *64*

Mormor's Chicken *69*

Chicken and Avocado Casserole *70*

Norwegian Meatballs *70*

Boiled Beef with Herb Dumplings *72*

Roald's Oxtail Stew *73*

Beef Royal *74*

Beef and Pickled Walnut Pie *76*

Tessa's Stuffed Lamb *81*

Latticed Lamb and Apricot Roulade with
Onion Sauce *82*

Paschal Lamb with Turnips *83*

Irish Stew *84*

Roast Loin of Pork with Hazelnut
Stuffing *84*

Marius's Ham *85*

Norwegian Fish Pudding *89*

Grilled Lobsters with Hot Herb Butter *91*

Spiv's Adaptation of Koulibiaka *92*

Salmon Fishcakes with Dill Sauce *92*

Monkfish with Leek and Lime Sauce *94*

Paella Salad *97*

Spiv's Favourite Pasta Sauce *97*

Fran Collins's Pasta Sauce *98*

Moussaka-type Lasagne *98*

'Savoury Crocodile' *100*

## *A Fine Dinner*

*R.D.* The other day Josie returned from a weekend with her parents in Suffolk and brought back with her three brace of partridge. As they had already been hung, we decided to have them that night. We invited my two sisters, Alfhild and Else, to join us, so the party consisted of Liccy and me, Theo, Josie, Alf and Else.

No fancy stuff with good young partridges, we all agreed. Just roasted plain.

I am not, on the whole, a Burgundy-drinking person, but I was aware that there were two very special bottles that had been down in the cellar for a long time, too long a time probably for Burgundy. One was the last bottle of the finest Burgundy I have ever tasted, a Chambolle Musigny (Grivelet) 1970, domaine-bottled and numbered. The other was a Musigny (Clair-Deu) 1970. So they were both nineteen years old, which is stretching it a bit for a Burgundy. We'll have them tonight, I told myself, and fetched them up.

In the glass they both surprised me. The colour, in each case, was deep red, almost purple, with not the slightest sign of paleness or browning, but the Chambolle was something to dream about. It must have been the combination of a perfect wine with absolutely perfect food that made this meal something none of us will ever forget.

The roast partridges were served on *croûtes* with breadcrumbs and bread sauce and gravy, accompanied by superbly cooked Brussels sprouts and game chips. The dessert was home-made vanilla ice cream with flambé bananas laced with Grand Marnier (see Rose's Cajun Vanilla Bananas, p. 174).

It was, we all agreed, the perfect meal. Here now is a description of another, contributed spontaneously by Alf, my ancient sister.

## A Feast to be Remembered

### ALFHILD HANSEN

During the war my mother and two of her daughters, Else and I, lived in a small thatched cottage in a fairly remote village called Grendon Underwood in Buckinghamshire. We were surrounded by farms and farmers and we got to know a number of them pretty well, but especially the Curtis family. And it was a great occasion when Mrs Curtis invited the three of us to supper. Rationing was fierce in those times and people like us were lucky to get an egg, a pint of milk and three ounces of butter a week. Naturally there were rumours that farmers were able to look after themselves very well in this regard, and who could blame them? So as we walked through the cold winter night to the Curtis farmhouse we all wondered whether at last we were going to find out just how well off the farmers were.

When the farmhouse door was opened, we were assailed by a delicious smell of food and a feeling of warmth and the sight of happy, smiling faces. Everything Mrs Curtis cooked was done on a large old iron range. The food Mrs Curtis laid on the table knocked us and our war-rationed stomachs clean over sideways. There were two plump Aylesbury ducks stuffed with herbs from her garden, home-made bread and butter, and roast potatoes, all crisp and brown, and apple sauce deliciously flavoured with cloves. As if that wasn't enough, the next course was a huge, steaming apple pie accompanied by lashings of thick rich, yellow cream. Real cream! We couldn't believe it! And to go with it all there was Mrs Curtis's powerful home-made rhubarb wine poured into big beakers. Then Mr Curtis rose from the table and sat down at the ancient upright piano and accompanied himself in 'Cockerels and Muscles, Alive Alive-oh'. It was a truly memorable meal, coming as it did right in the middle of the dreadful war, and I will never forget it.

## Roast Partridges with Juniper Stuffing

JOSIE

Serves 6

STUFFING

18 juniper berries

6 oz cooked ham, roughly chopped

3 medium onions, roughly chopped

zest of 2 lemons

4 oz butter

1 egg

dried marjoram

5 oz soft white breadcrumbs

salt and pepper, to taste

THE BIRDS

6 partridges

1 lemon

12 rashers streaky bacon

3 oz butter

4 fl oz dry white wine

about 1½ pt game or chicken stock

1 onion, sliced

1 bay leaf

6 slices bread, crusts removed

butter for frying the bread in

a little cornflour

salt and pepper

GARNISH

a bunch of watercress, washed

1. Preheat the oven to 375°F / 190°C / Gas mark 5.
2. Crush the juniper berries.
3. In a food processor blitz the roughly chopped ham and onion briefly.
4. Transfer the mixture to a bowl and add the lemon zest and melted butter.
5. Beat the egg and mix in along with the marjoram, breadcrumbs and seasoning.
6. Place the stuffing in the birds' cavities.
7. Place the partridges in a roasting pan and squeeze the lemon juice over them.
8. Bard them with streaky bacon, melt the butter and brush it over.
9. Pour in the wine and 6 fl oz game or chicken stock, add the onion and bay leaf, and roast for 30 minutes, basting often with the stock.
10. Remove the strips of bacon and roast for a further 15 minutes to brown the birds.
11. Meanwhile, fry the slices of bread in hot butter until golden brown.
12. When the birds are cooked, rest each on the *croûte* of fried bread. Place on a serving dish and keep warm while you make the gravy.
13. Skim off any fat. Mix cornflour with a little of the remaining stock and add to the roasting pan with the rest of the stock, stirring well. Bring to the boil and simmer, stirring and scraping off any sediment to add flavour.
14. When the correct consistency is reached (it should be fairly thin), season, strain and place in the gravy boat.

Garnish the birds with the watercress. Serve also with fried breadcrumbs and game chips.

## Casseroled Ptarmigan

ELSE LOGSDAIL

This was always a great treat when we arrived in Norway for our summer holidays and went to dinner at our grandparents' house in Oslo. It was a very festive occasion. Our grandfather sat in his rocking chair contentedly smoking his long pipe. Our aunts were out on the veranda sorting through large bowls of raspberries with a sewing needle to make sure there were no maggots in the fruit, and our grandmother bustled around everywhere. Wonderful smells wafted out of the kitchen and when we finally went in to eat, the table was glittering in the candlelight with all their lovely old silver and glass, and our grandfather made a little speech of welcome.

As ptarmigan is not easy to get in this country, old grouse makes a very good substitute.

Serves 4

4 rashers bacon

4 birds

6 oz butter

2 pt water

2 pt milk

pinch of salt

2 lumps sugar

1 slice Gjetost: Norwegian brown goat's-milk cheese (optional)

3 oz flour

2 tsp Bovril

1. Tie 1 rasher of bacon over the breast of each bird.
2. Melt 3 oz butter in a heavy saucepan or casserole and brown each bird well all over.
3. Bring the water and the milk to boil, then pour over the birds gradually. Making sure the saucepan lid is not fully on, simmer very slowly until tender for 2–3 hours, depending on the age of the birds. In the last 30 minutes add salt, sugar and Gjetost.
4. Remove birds and strain stock.
5. Make gravy in another pan. Melt remaining butter and add the flour. Blend well together and gradually add the stock. Add the Bovril, taste and adjust seasoning.
6. Replace birds in a casserole and pour gravy over them.

Serve with small roast potatoes, a green vegetable and *tittibaer*, a cranberry jelly.

## Jugged Hare

MARIUS BARRAN

First catch your hare. I first killed a hare when I was fourteen. My brother Julian and I were being taught to shoot in Somerset by the keeper of a local landowner, Lord Hilton. Using a ·410 shotgun, after numerous failures, with the help of the keeper, I shot a hare in a stubble field.

A week later, cooked by my mother, it was delicious. More recently I have cooked and eaten many hares, some of which I have shot, some picked up on the road and some bought. The great thing is to know how old the hare was when it died and how long it has been dead. A young hare, distinguishable by smaller size, slender shape and a small bony projection on the foreleg above the paw, may need to hang only three to four days. An older hare, without this bump, larger and heavier in the body, weighing up to 10 lb, may be hung for seven to ten days. The hare is hung up by the hind legs in a cool place with its head in a plastic bag to catch the blood, which should be kept for cooking later. If you buy a hare at the butcher, ask him how long ago it was killed. The size of the hare will determine how many people the recipe will serve.

## MARINADE

It is generally a good idea to marinate the hare, and a number of ingredients are suitable for this.

Place the pieces of hare in a cast-iron or earthenware pot and add 5 fl oz olive oil, 3 tbsp cider vinegar, or the juice of 1 lemon, ½ glass red wine, 5–6 cloves chopped garlic, juniper berries, bay leaf, thyme, pepper and salt. Hare is very dry meat. You may wish to increase the quantities of lemon and garlic, as these both improve the meat most effectively. Cover the pot and leave it for 12–24 hours, turning the pieces at least once during this period.

## TO COOK THE HARE

Chop 2–3 onions, and fry them gently in a mixture of 1¾ oz salted butter and 1¼ fl oz olive oil. Add 3½ oz fat bacon, chopped. Add the pieces of hare, the heart, liver, lungs and kidneys (these innards will not be particularly good to eat, but all add to the quality of the juices). Turn the meat until the pieces of hare have browned on both sides. Pour half a bottle of red wine (this may be as cheap as you can find, so long as it is not sour) over the meat. When it is hot, add the preserved blood and stir until it is steaming, but do not boil.

Preheat the oven to 400°F / 200°C / Gas mark 6. Add enough of the marinade to cover the pieces of hare and put the pot, with lid, into the oven. Leave it to cook for 2 hours, but turn the meat over twice during this time and top up the liquid from the marinade or with a 50/50 wine/water mix to keep the meat covered.

The hare should be served with the liquid poured over it, and sprinkled with a mixture of chopped coriander leaves, lemon peel and garlic. Redcurrant jelly (see recipe on p. 192) goes very well with it, as do root artichokes, chestnut purée, red cabbage (see recipe on p. 123) and baked potatoes. Nothing in the ingredients is fixed except the wine, the lemon juice, the garlic and the hare.

Good luck.

## *Thai Chicken*

PIP

The chicken breasts have to be marinated overnight.

Serves 6

### MARINADE
6 tbsp dark soy sauce
2 tbsp ground cumin
3 tbsp hot Madras curry powder
1 tbsp turmeric
3 cloves garlic, crushed
4 tbsp sweet chilli sauce
3 sticks lemon grass
5 fl oz oil
8 chicken breasts, boned

### FOR THE SAUCE
5 tbsp crunchy peanut butter
3 oz desiccated coconut, soaked in 6 fl oz boiling water
1 large bunch fresh coriander leaves, chopped

### GARNISH
8 oz bean sprouts
chopped coriander leaves

1. Mix all the marinade ingredients together, bruising the lemon grass with a knife handle.
2. Remove all traces of fat and skin from the chicken, cut into largish strips, add to the marinade and marinate overnight.
3. In a heavy saucepan, brown the marinated chicken *very* lightly over a medium heat; no additional oil is needed. Then add the peanut butter and most of the coconut and water.
4. Cover and simmer *very* slowly for about 20 minutes, finally adding some of the chopped coriander leaves (if more sauce is needed,

*Thai chicken*

add the remaining coconut and water). It is very important not to allow the chicken to cook too quickly or it will toughen.

Serve on a bed of rice, stick noodles or stir-fried rice, and garnish liberally with bean sprouts and chopped coriander leaves.

## *Chicken and Yoghurt Cream Curry*

PRUE LEITH

Serves 4

3-lb chicken

flour mixed with salt, pepper and 1 tsp each of turmeric, cayenne, dried English mustard and crushed coriander seeds

2 tbsp oil

2 medium onions, chopped

1 clove garlic, crushed

1 tsp cumin powder

2 tsp turmeric

10 fl oz chicken stock

1 bay leaf

2 tsp tomato purée

juice of 1 lemon

2 tsp chopped fresh mint

salt and pepper

1 tbsp single cream

2 tbsp plain yoghurt

1 oz blanched almonds

1. Preheat oven to 350°F / 180°C / Gas mark 4.

2. Joint the chicken into eight pieces and dip the pieces in the flour.

3. Heat the oil in a pan and fry the chicken pieces to seal them. Place the chicken in a casserole.

4. Now, in the same frying pan, fry the onions and garlic until brown.

5. Add the cumin and turmeric and cook for 2 minutes.

6. Add the stock, bay leaf, tomato purée, lemon juice and mint.

7. Taste and add salt and pepper as required.

8. Bring slowly to the boil, stirring continuously.

9. Pour this sauce over the chicken pieces, cover and cook in the oven for 45–50 minutes.

10. Lift the chicken pieces out and keep warm. Meanwhile, heat the curry sauce, adding the cream, yoghurt and almonds.

11. Replace the chicken pieces in the sauce and serve with boiled rice and a green salad.

# *My Mother*

*R.D.* My mother, Sofie Magdalene Hesselberg, was a Norwegian, as was my father. My mother's mother had an interesting surname for a Norwegian: it was Wallace (pronounced in Norway as Vallass). The Wallace family in Norway is directly traceable back to the Scottish national hero of the thirteenth century, Sir William Wallace. At the age of only twenty-seven, in 1297, he defeated the English at Stirling Castle and drove them out of Scotland, giving the Scots a glorious eight years of independence. Then the English King Edward sent up a great army and defeated the Scots and captured William Wallace. He was taken to London and executed and his family, who were hunted down mercilessly, escaped by boat to Bergen in Norway, where the Norwegian branch of the Wallaces was begun. Hence my grandmother, Ellen Wallace. I have a Wallace family tree with Sir William Wallace's name down in the roots and my own name and those of my sisters way up in the highest branch. All this is by the way, but I find it interesting.

My mother, Sofie (in Norway you pronounce the e at the end) was a smallish lady who, after she married my father, settled and lived most of her life in Wales and England. She bore five children and lost her eldest daughter from a ruptured appendix at the age of seven. A few months later, when I was only three, she lost her husband from pneumonia, and thereafter she devoted all her energy to raising her four children (Alf, Roald, Else and Asta, all still alive) as well as another two children from my father's previous marriage.

Mama died in 1967 at the age of eighty-two, when I was fifty. She was undoubtedly the absolute primary influence on my own life. She had a crystal-clear intellect and a deep interest in almost everything under the sun, from horticulture to cooking to wine to literature to paintings to furniture to birds and dogs and other animals – in other words, in all the interesting and lovely things in the world. Her hair, when she let it down, as she did every morning so that she could brush it assiduously, reached three-quarters of the way down her back, and it was always carefully plaited and coiled in a bun on the top of her head. She could cook a meal for twelve without turning a hair and her recipes, especially the Norwegian ones, were legion. Like all Norwegians, she preferred her fish to be simply poached and, again like the Norwegians, she ate all the skin of the boiled fish, be it black or white, saying that was where the best taste lay.

On our summer holidays in Norway she was an intrepid sailor. Over there we had a rowing boat and a small motorboat. She would think nothing of rowing us six children on an hour's journey to some outlying island for a swim, and in the little motorboat she would take us out in the most outlandish gales and the boat would virtually stand on its end as my mother, grasping the tiller, guided it over the crests of the massive waves. There was no nonsense about wearing life-jackets in those days. We simply clung on to the sides of the boat, cheering her on and getting soaked to the skin. In that way she taught us to be totally fearless and always treat dangerous situations as great adventures.

Each one of her four children, even when they were married, settled within a few miles of our mother when she was alive. She was the matriarch, the materfamilias, and her children radiated round her like planets round a sun. In some families children rebel and go as far away as possible from the parents, especially after they are married, because mothers-in-law are not always popular in the household. But with Mama's children and their marriage partners there was a genuine desire to keep this remarkable old parent within reach. There were a number of reasons for this. Although she had a

powerful personality, she never exercised her power. It lay dormant and was never a threat. She was a fount of wisdom and experience and would give sound advice whenever it was asked for, but she would never throw her advice around or give it *unless* you asked for it. She never criticized her grown-up children, however much they deserved it, so you knew you could go to see her at any time and your misdeeds would not be mentioned. Nor did she indulge in that favourite occupation of many mothers and mothers-in-law, which is to criticize the behaviour of her grandchildren. She might frown a little when a grandchild was ill-mannered, but she would never voice her disapproval. She expected the parents to do that. Nor would she ever try to tell me or my sisters how to run our lives, but we all knew that whenever we wanted help, which we often did, she would give it freely and wisely. In other words, she had the secret of holding her family close together, and that, I may tell you, is a rare gift indeed. So you can see why it was always a pleasure to live near her and to visit her, and we would all drop in more than once a week.

A golden rule of hers was never to spend the night in the house of a friend or even in the house of one of her married children. Rather than do this she would go to a hotel. I must say I totally agree with her. I have never felt completely comfortable staying in anyone else's house and I hate having to use other people's bathrooms.

My mother was widely read. She read the great Norwegian writers in their own language, Ibsen, Hamsun, Undsett and the rest of them, and in English she read the writers of her time, Galsworthy, Arnold Bennett, Kipling, etc. When we were young, she told us stories about Norwegian trolls and all the other mythical Norwegian creatures that lived in the dark pine forests, for she was a great teller of tales. Her memory was prodigious and nothing that ever happened to her in her life was forgotten. Embarrassing moments, funny moments, desperate moments were all recounted in every detail and we would listen enthralled.

Her general knowledge was startling, and she kept a fine old set of leather-bound *Encyclopaedia Britannica*, thirty-two volumes in all, near at hand so she could read about anything she didn't know. I have inherited these and use them often. She knew about birds and boats and bees and she treasured her paintings and fine furniture. But above all she knew about plants and vegetables, cooking and gardening, and a great deal of this knowledge rubbed off on her children. I myself have vivid childhood memories of many of my mother's dishes. Here are a couple.

Cauliflower and Shrimps, or in Norwegian, *Blomkaal med reker*. This simple dish, which is very Norwegian, has always remained the most abiding memory of all the meals that my mother prepared for us as children. We simply loved it. And it is one of the healthiest foods a parent can give to the family. See p. 106 for the recipe.

Boiled Hen in a Dish. This was perhaps my mother's most famous preparation and certainly one of the most remembered. It is difficult to get a boiler-hen these days, but they can be found. Once again, this is the simplest of foods, served in a large oval dish, with the meat neatly cut into parts with all skin removed, and with small boiled potatoes and *petits pois* and sometimes some onions and diced carrots, the whole thing swimming in a delicious pale sauce. I don't know how to make it myself, but all her daughters, granddaughters and great-granddaughters do, and you will find the recipe following.

## *Mormor's Chicken*

### LOU

This recipe is much more delicious than the name suggests. When I was away at boarding school, feeling hungry and longing for some good food, I would lie in bed dreaming of boiled chicken. When I came home for the holidays, my mother would always ask me what I wanted for my first meal at home and the answer would invariably be boiled chicken. In those days chicken was quite a luxury, as it was more expensive than other meats, but now this is a comparatively inexpensive meal and it is a great favourite with my own children. One great advantage is that it can be prepared the day before and reheated gently in the oven. I usually prepare the chicken a day in advance, but make the sauce before serving, as it tends to thin on reheating.

Serves 6

1 boiling chicken
$1\frac{1}{2}$ lb carrots
2 medium onions, sliced
bouquet garni
1 chicken stock cube
14-oz can potatoes
8 oz frozen peas

salt and pepper, to taste
$1\frac{1}{2}$ oz butter
$1\frac{1}{2}$ oz flour
1 pt stock from chicken
10 fl oz milk

1. Place the chicken in a large saucepan and almost cover with water.
2. Slice some of the carrots and put in the pan along with the onions.
3. Add the bouquet garni, salt and pepper and the stock cube.
4. Bring to the boil and simmer for 2 hours or more until the chicken is tender.
5. About 30 minutes before the end add the remaining carrots and potatoes.
6. Add the peas at the last moment.
7. Take the chicken and vegetables out of the pan and cool.
8. Strain the liquid and use as stock for the sauce.
9. Melt the butter in a pan, add the flour and cook on a low heat for 1–2 minutes. Draw aside, add the stock, blend and return to the heat and stir until it thickens. Season with salt and pepper and add the milk. Bring to the boil and cook for several minutes or until syrupy in consistency.
10. When the chicken is cool enough to handle, remove the flesh from the carcass and discard the skin.
11. Add the chicken and vegetables to the sauce and heat through, stirring occasionally. Taste and correct the seasoning and serve.

## Chicken and Avocado Casserole

### CALLIE

The chicken can be poached in advance and the stock reserved.

Serves 6

6-lb chicken cut into four pieces (or 2×3-lb chickens, jointed)

2 pt water

1 medium onion, peeled and quartered

2–3 stalks celery, roughly chopped

1 tbsp salt

peppercorns

2 carrots, peeled and roughly chopped

1 bay leaf

2 oz butter

$1\frac{1}{2}$ oz flour

8 fl oz single cream

2 oz grated strong cheese

fresh chopped rosemary

fresh chopped basil

salt

hot pepper sauce, e.g. Tabasco

6 oz mushrooms

2 large ripe avocados

GARNISH

2 oz flaked almonds, roasted

1. Put chicken pieces into a large pot with the water, onion, celery, salt, peppercorns, carrots and bay leaf. Bring up to the boil and simmer gently, skimming frequently. Simmer for about 2 hours or until the chicken is tender (the meat should fall off the bone easily).
2. Remove from the pan and cool.
3. When cool enough to handle, remove meat from the bones (except wings), put the bones, skin and wings back into the pan and simmer for another 30 minutes.
4. Strain stock (you should have about $1\frac{1}{4}$ pt) and cool.
5. Preheat oven to 350°F / 180°C / Gas mark 4.
6. In a saucepan melt $1\frac{1}{2}$ oz butter and stir in the flour.
7. Stir in the stock, cream, cheese, herbs, salt and hot pepper sauce. Stir until the sauce thickens and comes to the boil.
8. Clean and halve or quarter the mushrooms, depending on size. Sauté them in the remaining butter.
9. Place mushrooms and chicken in the bottom of a casserole, season and pour over the sauce. Cover and bake for 25 minutes or until the chicken is heated through.
10. Slice the avocados, place in the casserole, cook for about 10 minutes until avocado is warmed through.
11. Just before serving, sprinkle the roasted almonds on top.

## Norwegian Meatballs

### JOSIE

This dish is traditionally served with boiled cabbage and boiled potatoes.

Makes 16 meatballs

$1\frac{1}{2}$ oz fresh white breadcrumbs

salt and pepper

1 tbsp Worcestershire sauce

1 tbsp each chopped fresh thyme, parsley and chives

1 egg, beaten

$1\frac{1}{2}$ lb fillet steak, minced once

a little beef dripping for frying

14½-oz can good quality beef consommé

3 fl oz white wine

*beurre manié*, made with 1 oz butter and 2 tbsp flour

5 fl oz sour cream

GARNISH

chopped parsley

1. In a bowl mix gently the breadcrumbs, salt and pepper, Worcestershire sauce, herbs and egg into the meat.

2. Take a tablespoon of the mixture and, with floured hands, gently mould into meatballs. Take care not to compact the meat too tightly.

3. Fry the meatballs in the hot dripping to seal them and then lower the heat to cook the meat through, about 10–15 minutes. The meatballs should not be dry and therefore can be served medium-rare in the centre.

4. The meatballs can also be barbecued on a narrow-wired grill plate.

5. Bring the beef consommé and the white wine to the boil and whisk in the *beurre manié* until the consistency of a sauce is reached. Season and add sour cream.

6. Taking care not to break the meatballs, add the sauce, coating them with it.

Serve sprinkled with chopped parsley.

## Boiled Beef with Herb Dumplings

### CLARE

Give your butcher 3–4 days' notice so that he can cure the meat for you. It's perfect to serve to a group of hungry men.

Serves 6–8

4 lb salted silverside

1 bay leaf

bouquet garni, made with a small bunch of parsley stalks and a few sprigs of thyme

about 6 peppercorns

1 medium onion studded with cloves

1½ lb carrots, peeled and cut into 1½-in. lengths

1½ lb turnips, peeled and quartered

1 lb shallots, peeled

HERB DUMPLINGS

4 oz self-raising flour, sifted

4 oz fresh breadcrumbs

4 oz shredded suet

2–3 tbsp fresh mixed herbs, such as thyme, parsley, rosemary, marjoram

2 eggs, lightly beaten

salt and pepper

1. Place the beef into a large pan and cover with cold water.
2. Bring slowly to the boil and skim frequently.
3. Add the bouquet garni, peppercorns and studded onion.
4. Half-cover the pan and simmer for 1¾ hours.
5. Meanwhile, make the dumplings. Mix together flour, breadcrumbs, suet, freshly chopped herbs, eggs and seasoning. Divide equally into small dumplings, shaped by the palms of your hands.
6. Remove bouquet garni and studded onion from pan, and skim.
7. Add the carrots, turnips and shallots.
8. Bring back to the simmer and cook for a few minutes.
9. Carefully add the dumplings. They will sink at first. Cover with the lid and allow to cook for about 40 minutes, until the dumplings are light and fluffy.

To serve, carefully remove the dumplings from the pan and place on a carving board. Now remove the meat from the pan and put on the board. Strain out the vegetables and place in a serving dish. Strain any fat off the cooking liquor and serve with the meat.

## *Roald's Oxtail Stew*

*R.D.* Despite the fact that I am a very ordinary cook indeed, my oxtail stew, every time I make it, is greeted with exclamations of relish and sometimes even loud applause. By some fluke rather than by any real skill it always seems to come out right. So, for what it is worth, I shall tell you as best I can how I make it.

1. Always buy more than you think you'll need. Oxtail is so delicious that most people are inclined to ask for second and even third helpings. I allow one tail for every three guests, and if I'm feeding nine or ten, I will always buy four. Ask the butcher to chop them up. Most good butchers keep oxtail in stock frozen rather than fresh, but it makes no difference.

2. Always trim off fat and gristle.

3. I don't bother to brown them in fat before boiling. I've come to the conclusion it makes little difference. Simply bung all the oxtail

pieces into a large saucepan, cover them with water and get the whole thing boiling gently. Shove in a lot of beef stock cubes, six at least.

4. The main secret of this dish is to make absolutely sure that the meat is very well cooked. It should be almost falling off the bone when served. This will require roughly 4 hours' boiling. Towards the end, keep taking out a piece and testing it.

5. While the tails are cooking, boil some carrots and then purée them in the blender or food processor. This will ultimately be the only thickener you use for the liquid. No flour.

6. About 15 minutes from the end, throw in plenty of medium-sized onions.

7. Examine your bottles of dried herbs and make an instinctive selection, choosing the ones you yourself particularly like. Perhaps rosemary, basil and mixed herbs. Use liberally.

8. Three minutes from the end add whatever frozen vegetables you have. I favour broad beans, sweet corn and peas. The quantity of each that you use is a matter for your own judgement.

9. Lastly, thicken the liquid with your purée of carrots.

You should now have a lovely, rich, pungent oxtail stew. Serve in soup plates with plenty of hot French bread. Have a large dish on the table into which people can throw their used bones.

As you can see, this oxtail stew recipe is about as vague and imprecise as a recipe could be. But it is fun to cook like that, using your own judgement all the time, throwing in a bit of this and a bit of that, tasting it constantly and never consulting the cookbook.

## Beef Royal

### PENNY MINTO

This Elizabethan dish is really delicious. It should be made the day before you want it and eaten cold, which brings out the excellent flavour. It is very good for a buffet lunch or supper. We often serve it on Boxing Day.

Serves 12+

4–5 lb sirloin of beef, boned; keep the bones for stock

1 pig's foot or ½ calf's foot

½ bottle white wine

salt and pepper, to taste

cloves, mace and nutmeg, grated, to taste

grated rind of ½ lemon

2 tbsp fresh chopped marjoram

6 gammon rashers, sliced thinly

1 oz butter

1 bay leaf

1 glass port

3 filleted anchovies, pounded

3 pickled walnuts, chopped

If you are unable to get the pig's or calf's foot, use 1 level tbsp aspic jelly to every 10 fl oz of stock. This will not have quite the flavour, but will give you a jelly.

1. Cook the beef bones with the pig's or calf's foot in the white wine and a little water to cover, with salt and pepper, until you have a good broth. Let it get cold before straining.

2. Cut six incisions into the beef, being careful to leave the meat in one piece, and beat the flaps, taking great care not to tear them off.

3. On top of each flap of meat put a sprinkling of the cloves, mace, nutmeg, lemon rind, marjoram, salt and pepper, then lay a strip of gammon on top. Do this for each incision, then skewer well and tie it up thoroughly so that it does not fall apart in cooking.

4. Melt the butter in a frying pan and brown the meat on all sides. Put into a large saucepan or casserole, add the bay leaf and the strained broth. Cook very gently, covered, for 3–4 hours. Let it cool before taking out the meat. Put the meat into the deep dish it will be served from.

5. Remove any fat from the stock, add the port and the pounded anchovies, then boil and let it bubble well for about 8–10 minutes. When slightly cooled, add the chopped pickled walnuts and pour the sauce gently over and around the beef. Put in a cold place until the jelly has set.

When serving, cut the jelly into cubes and serve with the sliced meat.

## Beef and Pickled Walnut Pie

### PIP

The pie filling should be made a day in advance.
You will need a 4-pt or 12 × 8-in. pie dish.

Serves 6

FILLING
cooking oil
1 large onion, chopped
2 cloves garlic, crushed
3 rashers smoked streaky bacon, chopped
3 lb lean beef, cubed
2 tbsp flour
1 beef stock cube, crumbled
1 glass red wine
1 tbsp strong mustard
1 tbsp tomato purée
1 tbsp mixed herbs
2 tbsp mushroom ketchup (optional)
2 tbsp Worcestershire sauce
8 oz mushrooms, washed and halved
12 pickled walnuts, halved
2 tbsp chopped parsley
salt and pepper, to taste

PASTRY
1 lb puff pastry
1 egg, beaten

1. Heat a little oil in a heavy saucepan, add the onion, garlic and bacon and cook till soft. Set aside.

2. In a separate pan, heat some more oil and brown the beef in batches, then add to the onion and bacon mixture.

3. Sprinkle the flour over the beef and return to a medium heat. Stir in the stock cube, red wine, mustard, tomato purée, herbs, mushroom ketchup and Worcestershire sauce.

4. Cover and simmer *very* slowly for approximately 2 hours or until the meat is tender.

5. Add the mushrooms and pickled walnuts and gently stir in the parsley. Season with salt and pepper. Allow to cool in the saucepan, preferably overnight.

6. The following day preheat the oven to 350°F / 180°C / Gas mark 4.

7. Roll out the pastry. Using the pie dish as a guide, cut the pastry ½ in. larger all round than the rim of the dish. Then cut an extra ½-in. width of pastry to make a double layer round the rim. Use the remaining pastry to cut decorative leaves.

8. Place the cooked pie filling in the dish, with a pie funnel or upturned egg cup in the centre.

9. Lightly grease the rim of the pie dish. Place the ½-in. width of pastry around the rim and brush with beaten egg. Then cover with the measured pastry and brush with beaten egg. Flute the edges with a sharp knife and decorate the top with pastry leaves brushed with beaten egg.

10. Bake for 20–30 minutes until the pastry is well risen and golden.

*Beef and pickled walnut pie*

*The hall, Gipsy House: Easter feast*

Easter Feast

Easter Rabbit Soup with Horns of Plenty

The Paschal Lamb with Turnips
White Sprouting Broccoli
Potatoes & Onions with Cream & Garlic

Curd Cheese Tarts
First Rhubarb of the Year
Easter Cakes

## *Easter*

*R.D.* Easter is as lovely as Christmas is horrible. There is no serious present-giving, just a few eggs to the children and a bunch of flowers for him or her, but that (unless you live in Russia) is the end of it. Everyone who feels that Christmas is wonderful should study his feelings at Easter and compare the two. There are none of those awful present-buying pressures as Easter Day draws near, no tree-buying, no excessive eating and drinking. The only organized ritual is the Easter-egg hunt in the garden for the children and that is nothing but fun. I used to love those hunts when I was very small. I think all children who are lucky enough to have a garden feel the same way. It is a simple procedure but when you are a child there is something incredibly exciting in finding a chocolate egg wrapped in silver paper cunningly hidden in the tuft of the heather plant or in the branches of ivy or in the bole of a hollow tree.

For the Easter holidays my mother always somehow managed to transport our entire family of six children to Tenby in Pembrokeshire. She rented one floor of a house called 'The Cabin', which was built on the stone pier of the Old Harbour, and at high tide the sea would literally smash against the stones below our windows. In Tenby we went for long walks along the tops of the cliffs and picked huge bunches of primroses. We gathered winkles on the rocks and cooked them and got them out of their shells with bent pins and had them for tea on slices of bread and butter. Sometimes we went for donkey-rides on the beach and once every Easter we took the boat across the water to Caldy Island to stare at the Benedictine monastery there and to wonder about the monks and how they ever managed to keep their vow of silence.

A super time was Easter when we were young. It is a super time now when we are old.

# My Lambs

## TESSA

Although I am now a very responsible young woman of thirty-two and a mother of three to boot, I will admit that as a child I was often a severe pain in the you-know-what to my elders and particularly to my father, who was then in charge of us children. And any mention of the word 'lamb' conjures up to him, I know, memories of an unpleasant incident that I engineered in one of my silliest moods at the age of about ten. I shall tell you about it briefly.

I went to stay the weekend with a schoolfriend who lived in Kent. While there we visited a sheep-farmer who had a lot of lambs. I immediately decided, in my usual unthinking way, that I wanted two lambs to take home with me (shades of Veruca Salt), and I bought them there and then with all my pocket money, telling my hosts that my father loved lambs and we had lots of sheep at home. All lies.

The lambs (they were actually almost sheep that I was given, large, clumsy, and not very clean) were put on leads made of baling-string and I persuaded the guard of the train up to London to take them in the guard's van and let me in with them. At Charing Cross I somehow got them into a taxi and we were driven to Marylebone to get the train to Great Missenden. Once again I got them into the guard's van, where they made a disgusting mess on the floor.

None of this was easy. You try crossing London with a couple of young sheep on bits of string, especially when you are ten years old, but I had a lot of nerve in those days.

Daddy met me at Great Missenden station and I won't repeat what he said when he saw what I had brought with me. He said worse things when we had to shove these creatures on to the beautiful leather back seats of his new Rover, but we got them back to Gipsy House and there they were put in the front garden, which was the only totally fenced-in piece of land we had. Very soon they had eaten everything in sight: the double border of white polyantha bush roses, the lobelia borders and a jackmanii clematis that had taken several years to train up an old apple tree.

Daddy said, 'That's it. They've got to go.'

'I won't have you sending them to a butcher!' I cried.

'Don't worry,' he said. 'Just get the leads on them tonight as soon as it gets dark.'

'Where are you taking them?' I shouted. 'I insist they go to a good home.'

'Sheep are not domestic animals,' he said. 'Have them ready to travel after supper tonight.'

That evening Daddy and I pushed and shoved the reluctant sheep down the lane until it met the main road about 600 yards away. We got them across the road and then turned left and went through a gate that led into a large field owned by some farmer we did not know. The field was full of sheep.

'Now let them loose,' Daddy said. 'They'll be fine in here.'

I undid the string around their necks and kissed them a tearful goodbye.

'That chap's going to be a bit puzzled the next time he counts his sheep,' Daddy said as we walked home.

'What will happen to them?'

'In due course they'll go to market with all the others,' Daddy said. 'You'll probably be eating one of them next time we have a leg of lamb.'

'Don't!' I cried. 'I'll never eat lamb again!'

Here is my lamb recipe. It's awfully good.

## Tessa's Stuffed Lamb

Serves 6

1 oz butter

3 oz fresh white breadcrumbs

1½ oz sultanas

1½ oz raisins

3 oz chopped walnuts

zest of 1½ oranges

1 tsp dried rosemary

1 tsp dried thyme

salt and pepper, to taste

juice of ½ orange

4-lb leg of lamb, boned but not rolled

1 large onion

GLAZE

2 oz soft brown sugar

juice of ½ lemon

juice of ½ orange

2 tbsp Worcestershire sauce

SAUCE

4 fl oz red wine

10 fl oz lamb stock

GARNISH

watercress

1. Preheat oven to 375°F / 190°C / Gas mark 5.

2. Peel and finely chop the onion.

3. Melt the butter in a pan and fry the onion for 3 minutes.

4. In a bowl mix together the fried onion, breadcrumbs, sultanas, raisins and walnuts.

5. Blend in the orange zest, rosemary, thyme, salt and pepper.

6. Bind together with the orange juice.

7. Sew up one end of the lamb. Stuff and then sew up the other end. Place in a greased roasting pan and roast for 1¾–2 hours, basting regularly.

8. About 15 minutes before the end of cooking, mix the glaze ingredients together, spoon over the lamb and continue to cook.

9. Remove meat from the roasting pan and keep warm. Drain off any fat from the juices.

10. Add the wine and lamb stock to the juices. Boil vigorously, scraping the bottom of the pan until the sauce is thickened. Correct seasoning and pour into a gravy boat.

Place the lamb on a carving board, garnish with watercress and serve.

## Latticed Lamb and Apricot Roulade with Onion Sauce

PIP

Serves 6

cooking oil

2 lb lean lamb, cut into 1-in. cubes

1 medium onion, chopped

1 clove garlic, chopped

8 oz dried apricots, soaked in water only if very hard

1 tbsp thyme

1 tbsp ground cumin

1 tsp whole coriander seeds, crushed

1 oz fresh breadcrumbs

2 oz whole almonds, roughly chopped

2 eggs, beaten

1 lb puff pastry

3 tbsp chopped parsley

ONION SAUCE

1 onion

15 fl oz milk

5 cloves

1 bay leaf

4 black peppercorns

2 oz butter

2 oz flour

1 generous tsp Dijon mustard

salt and pepper, to taste

1 tbsp finely chopped parsley

1. Preheat oven to 350°F / 180°C / Gas mark 4.
2. Heat a little oil in a frying pan and lightly brown the lamb in batches. Put the cooked pieces on to crumpled kitchen paper towels to drain. When cool enough to handle, cut into $\frac{1}{4}$-in. pieces.
3. In the same pan soften the onion and garlic, adding a little extra oil if necessary.
4. In a bowl combine meat, onion, garlic, apricots, parsley, herbs, breadcrumbs, almonds and three quarters of the beaten eggs. Season with salt and pepper.
5. Roll out the pastry into a rectangle and place the lamb mixture down the centre, leaving enough pastry on either end to seal the roulade.
6. With a sharp knife, cut the pastry diagonally at $\frac{1}{4}$-in. intervals in a herring-bone pattern.
7. Brush edges of pastry with beaten egg.
8. Fold over the pastry strips alternately to overlap, producing a plaited effect. Pinch the ends together and turn under to seal the roulade. Glaze the roulade with beaten egg.
9. Place on a baking sheet in the oven for about 30 minutes, then reduce the temperature to 320°F / 160°C / Gas mark $2\frac{1}{2}$ for a further 15 minutes.
10. Meanwhile, make the onion sauce. Peel the onion and place it in a small saucepan. Cover with the milk and add the cloves, bay leaf and peppercorns. Bring to simmering point until the onion is soft. Remove from the heat, strain the milk and reserve. Chop the onion and set aside.
11. Make a roux with the butter and flour, slowly adding 10 fl oz of the milk. Stir constantly until the sauce thickens and coats the back of the spoon. If too thick, add a little more milk.
12. Add the mustard and season to taste with salt and pepper.
13. Add the chopped onion, allow to heat through, then add the parsley.
14. Using palette knives, carefully transfer the roulade to a clean tray or plate. Use a few pieces of kitchen paper towel to absorb any excess juices that may emerge from the edges.

Serve sliced with the onion sauce.

*Latticed lamb and apricot roulade with onion sauce*

## *Paschal Lamb with Turnips*

### MARWOOD YEATMAN

Serves 6–8

3-lb loin of lamb, boned and skinned, without
the breast

grated rind 1 orange and 1 lemon

8 oz fresh white breadcrumbs

flour

1 egg, beaten

salt and pepper, to taste

1. Lay the lamb out flat, skin side down.
2. Mix the grated orange and lemon rind with
3 tbsp breadcrumbs. Season and spread over
the meat, paying particular attention to the
crevices.

3. Roll up the lamb and secure with string every
couple of inches.

4. Dust with flour, glaze with the egg and coat
with the remaining breadcrumbs.

5. Brown all over in hot fat and bake for 1 hour
at 350°F / 180°C / Gas mark 4.

6. Remove from oven and leave to rest in a
warm place for 5–10 minutes.

7. Undo the string and carve in slices.

Serve with boiled turnips, white sprouting broccoli, and Potatoes and Onions with Cream and
Garlic (see p. 113).

## Irish Stew

### LICCY

To get the best results from this recipe, cook the meat in home-made stock or good-quality lamb stock cubes.

Serves 6

2½ lb potatoes, peeled and thickly sliced

12 best-end-of-neck or middle-neck chops

1½ onions, peeled and thickly sliced

2 tsp pearl barley for every layer

6 tbsp chopped parsley

salt and pepper, to taste

1. In a large saucepan put a layer of raw potato, then a layer of meat, then a layer of onions, 2 tsp pearl barley, about 1 tbsp chopped parsley and season with salt and pepper.

2. Repeat this layering until all the ingredients are used.

3. Barely cover with water or stock (approximately 2½ pts) and put on a very low heat with the lid on. Simmer gently for 3–4 hours. Check from time to time in case more liquid is needed.

    Alternatively, cook the stew slowly in the oven at 300–325°F / 150–170°C / Gas mark 2–3 for 3–4 hours, removing the lid 30 minutes before the end to crisp the potato.

This is best if sprinkled with chopped parsley, served in soup plates, accompanied by carrots and peas.

## Roast Loin of Pork with Hazelnut Stuffing

### VIRGINIA

Serves 6–8

STUFFING

4 oz hazelnuts

12 prunes

12 dried apricots, soaked in water only if very hard

1 lb sausage meat

4 tbsp chopped fresh sage

salt and pepper, to taste

2 eggs, beaten

4–5 lb boned loin of pork, with the rind scored; if using a smaller piece of meat, halve the stuffing ingredients

1 onion, sliced

1. Preheat oven to 400°F / 200°C / Gas mark 6.

2. To make the stuffing, roughly chop the hazelnuts, prunes and apricots.

3. Mix with the sausage meat, sage, salt and pepper.

4. Add enough of the eggs to bind the stuffing together, and mix well.

5. Lay the loin of pork flat. Place some stuffing on top, then roll neatly and tie. Rub salt into the rind.

6. Roll any left-over stuffing into balls and roast alongside the meat for 40 minutes.

7. Weigh the meat and calculate the cooking time: allow 25 minutes per 1 lb, plus 25 minutes. Place the meat on a roasting rack inside a roasting pan with enough water to cover the bottom of the pan and add the sliced onion. Cook for the calculated time.

8. Skim fat off roasting liquid and use for stock.

Serve with braised red cabbage.

# *Hams*

### MARWOOD YEATMAN

They have ham classes up north, at the shows in the dales and beyond, which can transform a tiny village. For a few days the tents dwarf the terraces and may be seen for miles, a Field of Cloth of Gold, but white, arranged on a crimson moor. The sheepdog trials start at noon. Then the steam train leaves, a 4-6-0. There is English country dancing – A Real Princess, The Queen Victoria, and Count Your Blessings – and a cricket match on a wicket like potted meat, with the local prodigy carting the bowling all over the place (Yorkshire are having a look at him).

In the huge, hot produce tent, between monster gooseberries and beetroot as big as your head, there will be up to a dozen hard, flat, honey-coloured hams laid out on a trestle table. They are in two categories, under and over 25 lb – 40, 60, even 70 pounders, from thirty score pigs. The pork must have been cured since the previous show, home fed, immaculately cut and rounded off, dry salted, mature and have plenty of fat. This is the class guaranteed to turn the heads of southerners and any Europeans stopping by who thought they knew York ham. Outside the Midlands and the north, you do not see meat like this any more.

I was admiring the exhibits when a woman asked me how they were judged.

'At the show? By looks,' I said. 'A well-cut ham is a work of art.'

She liked the one that had taken third prize. I told her it should have come top.

'Quite right, lad,' said a voice behind me, 'that ham's mine.'

And so I met the first of the remaining farmers and butchers who salt their own pork, every year for the next, when the weather cools, and helped him carry his trophy back to the car. I went to see him that evening after milking out on his fifty acres in the middle of the moor, not really near anywhere, as he had explained, at the end of a track exposed to the winds off the North Sea. By this time his ham was back in the scullery, hanging on the wall above a row of gum boots, and his wife was frying rashers of bacon from a belly piece, 3 inches thick, for their tea.

## *Marius's Ham*

### Serves 16–24

12-lb ham on the bone, soaked in cold water overnight and drained

1 pt Guinness

1 pt dry cider

5 fl oz white wine vinegar

8 oz molasses

8 oz soft brown sugar

10 peppercorns

12 juniper berries

2 bay leaves

2 onions

2 carrots

2 stalks celery

#### TO DECORATE

3 oz breadcrumbs mixed with 3 oz brown sugar

black pepper, to taste

cloves

1. Place the ham in a large pot with all the main ingredients and top up with water to just cover the ham. Simmer for $3\frac{1}{2}$ hours.
2. Preheat the oven to 375–400°F / 190–200°C / Gas mark 5–6.
3. Remove the skin from the ham and cut the fat in a chequerboard pattern. Coat with breadcrumbs and brown sugar, and black pepper. Stud with cloves. Bake for $1\frac{1}{2}$ hours.

# Mothers and Daughters

*R.D.* Although nearly every mother is a great cook in the eyes of her own children, she is usually no more than a competent producer of decent plain food. Young children have untrained and rather vulgar palates and, as the makers of baked beans and vegetable-oil ice cream have long since discovered, they prefer bland-tasting food to any other. When they grow up, these unfortunates shy away from subtle flavours and are perfectly happy in a world where all foods taste alike. That is why they smother their meat or fish either with tomato ketchup or with one of those bottles of brown sauce that grace the tables of so many of our cafés.

Some mothers, of course, are genuinely marvellous cooks and they are the salt of the earth. They not only provide endless delight for their families and friends but, most important of all, they invariably pass on their talents to their female offspring. It is a curious and recondite fact that nearly every daughter of a marvellous mother-cook turns out to be a marvellous cook herself. Great mother-cooks produce great daughter-cooks and so on *ad infinitum*. The kitchens of great mother-cooks are suffused with a glow of enthusiasm and competence, and the children are encouraged to come in to watch and learn. The kitchens of lousy mother-cooks on the other hand are usually chaotic and messy, and any child who ventures in is likely to be greeted with an 'Oh, do get out of my way! Can't you see I'm busy!' The daughters in these families stand little chance of becoming even half-way decent cooks. The kitchen is to them, as it was to their mothers, a place of frustration and hard labour.

Now Josie, who is already close to becoming a master cook at the age of twenty-one, breaks all the above rules. Her mother, the wife of a Suffolk farmer, has spent her married life satisfying the gigantic appetites of men who work hard out of doors in all weathers. She is therefore a sound producer of good wholesome satisfying food, but nobody, certainly not she herself, would claim that she is one of those amazing mother-cooks who is going to inspire her daughter to do great things in the kitchen. And so why, we have to ask ourselves, did Josie, out there on a Suffolk farm, at the tender age of sixteen, announce suddenly to a bemused family that she intended to take up cooking as a career?

I don't know the answer to that one. I can only guess that she must have been born with the gift and as she grew older the urge to make use of it began to assert itself. No art school is going to make an average artist into a great painter unless the talent is there, and for the same reason no cooking school is going to make an ordinary good cook into a Monsieur Boulestin. Quite obviously Josie has the gift. Cooking is in the tips of her fingers and in her blood, and whatever she touches in the kitchen comes out just that much better than you could ever have expected. She is a shining exception to my theory that all great daughter-cooks have great mother-cooks.

However, my own family and Liccy's (my mother with her three daughters and Liccy with *her* three daughters) support the theory 100 per cent. My mother was a superb cook. Being pure Norwegian, her cooking had naturally a powerful Scandinavian style. Her daughters (my sisters), Alfhild, Else and Asta, are all exceptional cooks and are contributors to this book. Liccy's late mother was a wonderful cook and Liccy, naturally, is magnificent. Her three daughters, Neisha, Charlotte and Lorina, are almost as good as their mother and that's saying something. They are also contributors to this book.

On our summer holidays in Norway we would often row out into the fjord in the early evenings to fish. We dropped anchor and baited our hooks with mussels and let out the lines until the weights hit the bottom. Then, unless we were after flat fish, we pulled our lines up two good arm-lengths above the sea-bed and waited. Each of us held the line in the proper manner around the back of the first finger with the thumb on top, and we sat very still, hardly daring to speak because, although the fjord was very deep, we weren't certain that the fish mightn't hear us. It is still a great mystery to me how even a tiny nibble on that bait, which is sometimes 200 feet down, will transmit itself sharply to one's fingers, but it always does. And oh, the excitement of it all when the good strong bite came and you would

jerk your hands upwards and yell, 'I've got one! . . . No, I haven't! . . . Yes, I have! I've got him all right!' And then you would have to stand up in the boat for the frantic hauling-in, and you would be peering over the side to see how big he was as he first came into view, a silver streak flashing to and fro down in the clear water. 'It's a whopper!' you'd shout. 'I've got a whopper!' But they always looked bigger under the water than they did when you got them out.

We caught small cod and whiting and haddock, but mostly it was those little codlings, about twelve inches long, and we rowed back with them to the rocky shore and cleaned them in the sea-water and carried them in to my mother. Within half an hour we were eating them for supper, gently fried in butter together with small boiled potatoes. I have never tasted fish as good as those baby cod, with their delicate flaky flesh and slightly crispy skin. They were glorious and we would eat three or four of them each, if we had caught enough. The secret, of course, was not so much in the cooking but in the fact that the fish were just about as fresh as fish could be. There is no recipe for it in this book. If you want it, you will have to go to Norway and catch it yourself in the fjord on a summer evening.

*Norwegian fish pudding*

## Norwegian Fish Pudding

### LOU

I remember my Norwegian grandmother making this dish for us many years ago before the advent of food processors. She laboriously scraped the fish from the skin by hand and it took a long time to prepare. Consequently, it was not made very often and it was a great treat. Now, of course, with the aid of a food processor it is very quick and simple to prepare. It makes a delicious light supper or an impressive dinner-party dish. I usually make this recipe with a prawn sauce but it is just as good with a number of other sauces, such as cheese, spinach, tomato or curry.

You will need six timbales or a 3-pt ring mould.

Serves 6

### PUDDING

8 oz smoked haddock (undyed)

8 oz smoked cod

10 fl oz milk

6 fl oz double cream

$1\frac{1}{2}$ tbsp potato flour

2 tsp salt

pepper

### SAUCE

$\frac{3}{4}$ oz butter

$\frac{3}{4}$ oz flour

10 fl oz milk

2 tsp tomato purée

1–2 tbsp sherry

juice of $\frac{1}{2}$ lemon approximately

3 oz smoked mussels and 3 oz smoked oysters or 6 oz peeled shrimps

### GARNISH

chopped parsley

6 shrimps in their shells

1. Skin the fish. Put the fish in a food processor and process for a few seconds. Mix in the milk, cream, potato flour, salt and pepper.

2. Put mixture into lightly oiled timbales or a small ring mould. Cover with kitchen foil and place in a roasting pan half-filled with water and bake at 400°F / 200°C / Gas mark 6 for about 20 minutes, until firm to touch.

3. Meanwhile, prepare the sauce. In a pan melt the butter and add the flour to make a roux, then gradually add the milk, stirring continuously to avoid lumps. Add the tomato purée, sherry and lemon juice to taste. Bring to the boil and cook for a few minutes. Season to taste.

4. Add the smoked mussels and oysters or the peeled shrimps. Allow them to heat through, but do not cook them.

5. When the pudding is cooked, ease around the edges of the mould with a sharp knife. Then place the serving dish on top of the mould, turn it upside-down quickly and the fish pudding should slide easily on to the dish.

6. Pour the sauce over the pudding, sprinkle with a little chopped parsley and garnish with the shelled shrimps.

Serve immediately with a watercress salad.

# The Bay of Galway

*R.D.* There is an enormous bookshop in the little town of Galway that is world famous. It is called Kenny's Bookshop, and people like Graham Greene order books from there. Every summer, Galway organizes a Children's Festival and for a week the entire town is turned over to entertaining children, who come from all over Ireland to join in. The streets are filled with clowns and other crazy performers, working from horse-drawn wagons, and on the pavements all sorts of competitions with sand and chalk and other things go on. I was invited over to contribute to the bookshop part of the festival a couple of years ago; Liccy of course came with me and so did my daughter Ophelia who is always such a pleasure to have around. I nearly killed myself signing books non-stop for three days, but on our last evening the three of us broke away and drove to a small restaurant on the shores of Galway Bay where they told us to order lobster.

We each received a massive, grilled crustacean that had literally just been brought in by the lobster-fishermen, and it was served with plain melted butter and crisp bread. I am not one of those who think lobster is a great dish, but I tell you these three, fresh out of the icy waters of the Bay and accompanied by a crackling cold bottle of good Fumé, that we ate in a quiet room overlooking the great calm sea, were astonishing and unforgettable. They were different lobsters to any we had ever had before. What is it that makes three lobsters for three people taste totally and utterly different from all the others one has eaten in a long life? It is of course partly the mood, the atmosphere, the still waters of the Bay and the blue hills beyond. But forgetting all that, each of us found ourselves saying that these were not lobsters but some kind of food of the gods that had been dropped gently on to our plates from the great kitchen in heaven. Each of us who is in the habit of tasting food with care has experienced this sort of a phenomenon now and again and it is always a wonderful surprise that really has no explanation.

Now and again, most of us are faced with the problem of boiling our own live lobsters, and because this caused me so much anguish and guilt, I made a study of all the inhuman things that people do to animals in order to eat them. I then wrote a story about it (*Pig*). We all know about the foie gras geese and the treatment of calves for veal production (I won't eat either), and I found a recipe from Florida that said, 'Surprise the terrapin by dropping it into boiling water . . .' But lobsters are what will concern most of us from time to time. So here is what I discovered years ago from a scientific RSPCA paper on the subject. The lobster has a comparatively highly developed central nervous system, and the usual method of simply dropping it into a pot of boiling water subjects it to at least forty seconds of intense torture. Sometimes you can even hear one screaming. The kindest way of overcoming this problem is this. While you are waiting for the water to boil, you take a basin of cold water and you dissolve into it half a pound of cheap kitchen salt or agricultural salt, making a strong saline solution. You then immerse the heads of the live lobsters in this for a minute or two, and presto, they become totally anaesthetized. That's the perfect way. Next best, if you don't have the salt, is to put the lobsters in cold water and bring it gently to the boil. The scientists have demonstrated that as the water gradually gets warmer and warmer, the lobsters simply drowse off gently without pain. So there you are. Take your pick.

## Grilled Lobsters with Hot Herb Butter

RICHARD STEIN

Serves 4

2 uncooked lobsters, each weighing about 2½ lb

Melted butter for basting the lobster

3 fl oz fish stock or water

1 oz chopped fresh herbs (equal quantities of chervil, chives and basil)

Juice of a quarter lemon

4 oz unsalted butter, cut into pieces

1. Preheat your grill.

2. To cut the lobster in half, place it on a chopping board and drive a large knife through the middle of the carapace (the body section) and cut down towards and between the eyes.

Then turn the knife around, place it in the original cut and bring the knife down right through the tail to split that in half. Pull off the claws, cut off the rubber bands that will be binding the claws, and crack open each of the three claw sections with a short, sharp chop from the thickest part of your knife blade.

3. Place the lobster, flesh side up, on a grilling tray and paint copiously with melted butter. Cook under the grill till the flesh has set, then turn over, brush with melted butter again and grill the shell side till it has turned from blue to red. Keep them in a warm place.

4. Bring the fish stock or water to the boil, then add the herbs and lemon juice. Remove from the heat and whisk in the butter, a piece at a time.

5. Pour the hot herb butter over the lobsters and serve.

## Spiv's Adaptation of Koulibiaka

A dish that can be made with either expensive specially bought ingredients (such as lobster or salmon) or left-over chicken. It always looks spectacular.

Serves 8

1 roll of filo pastry

1½ pt béchamel sauce with a pinch of nutmeg added

1½ lb cooked salmon *or* lobster *or* good smoked haddock *or* chicken and shrimps

4 hard-boiled eggs, sliced

red salmon caviar (optional; sometimes you have a lucky find in a whole salmon!)

SORREL SAUCE

large bunch of sorrel; if sorrel is not available, or for a change, make an extra 1 pt béchamel and add 1 tbsp anchovy essence

1 oz unsalted butter

salt and pepper, to taste

8 oz *fromage frais* (8% fat)

1. Preheat oven to 400°F / 200°C / Gas mark 6.

2. Choose an ovenproof dish and cut 4 pieces of pastry to fit. Cook the pastry, following the instructions on the package. Allow to cool.

3. Make the béchamel sauce, sprinkle a little milk on top to stop skin forming and set aside.

4. Now make the sorrel sauce. Remove stalks, wash sorrel leaves and roughly tear them. Melt the butter in a saucepan and sweat the leaves in it. Add salt and pepper. Allow to cool a little and beat in the *fromage frais*.

5. To assemble, place a sheet of pastry in the ovenproof dish, followed by half the béchamel and half the fish or chicken. Place a sheet of pastry on top of this, then the sorrel sauce and eggs, and shrimps if used. Then a sheet of pastry, followed by the remaining béchamel and fish or chicken, and caviar if used. Finish with a sheet of pastry.

6. Cover with kitchen foil and place in the oven for 20–25 minutes until piping hot.

Serve with a green salad.

## Salmon Fishcakes with Dill Sauce

PIP

These fishcakes go very well with the Baked Marinated Courgettes (p. 116).

Serves 8

FISHCAKES

12 oz salmon *or* 8 oz salmon and 4 oz cod

1 lb potatoes

1 oz butter

1 tsp chopped dill

a little chopped parsley

salt and pepper, to taste

a little fresh lemon juice

1 egg, beaten, for binding

a little flour

2 eggs, beaten, for coating

4 oz fresh breadcrumbs

vegetable oil for frying

*Salmon fishcakes with dill sauce*

DILL SAUCE

1 oz flour

1 oz butter

10 fl oz fish stock

10 fl oz single cream

2 tbsp lemon juice

1 large bunch of dill, finely chopped

2 tsp Dijon mustard

salt and pepper, to taste

GARNISH

dill

1. Poach and flake the fish. Reserve and reduce the poaching liquid for the stock.

2. Boil and mash the potatoes.

3. Mix together the fish, potatoes, butter, dill, parsley, salt and pepper and lemon juice, and bind with a little egg.

4. With floured hands, divide the mixture into 8.

5. Shape into flat, round, equal-sized cakes.

6. Coat them with the beaten egg and then the breadcrumbs.

7. To make the sauce, make a roux with the butter and flour. Gradually add the fish stock, bring to the boil and simmer for a couple of minutes. Add the cream, lemon juice, mustard and dill. Season to taste.

8. Heat the oil in a frying pan, and fry the fishcakes, turning once, until crisp and golden (or use deep-fat fryer). Drain well on absorbent kitchen paper towels.

9. Heat the dill sauce thoroughly and serve. Garnish with a sprig of dill.

# Monkfish with Leek and Lime Sauce

PIP

Serves 4

2 lb monkfish, thoroughly cleaned and cut into 1-in. cubes

salt and pepper, to taste

3 oz butter

4 leeks, washed and very thinly sliced

1 tbsp flour

5 fl oz fish stock

1 tsp dried *or* 2 tsp fresh tarragon

5 fl oz single cream

juice of 1 lime

GARNISH

1 lime, sliced

fresh tarragon leaves

1. Season the monkfish with salt and pepper and fry very briefly in batches in about 1 oz butter. Set aside.

2. Add the leeks to the frying pan with another 1 oz butter and soften. Season, set aside and keep warm.

3. Melt the remaining butter in the same frying pan, blend in the flour and then add the liquid that has emerged from the monkfish and most of the fish stock, stirring constantly.

4. As soon as the sauce begins to thicken, add the tarragon, the juice of 1 lime, and most of the cream.

5. Return the monkfish to the sauce with any further liquid that has emerged, and cook gently for a few minutes.

6. Season to taste, adding a little more fish stock and cream if necessary.

7. Arrange the leeks on a warmed serving dish and spoon on the monkfish and sauce.

*L.D.* Having been brought up in a Roman Catholic house, fish was served always on Fridays. I'm not sure whether this was for the benefit of the soul or the fishmonger. My father's favourite recipe was my mother's traditional fish pie: large flakes of haddock half smoked, half unsmoked, delicately poached in milk with dabs of butter, a bay leaf and a few peppercorns. A parsley sauce was made always with double quantities of chopped fresh parsley and the poaching liquid; sliced hard-boiled egg would be added to the pie and an exquisite mashed potato lightly piped round the edge. The most important feature of this pie was that every bone was removed. My mother had a strong belief that most children disliked fish because of the bones and I'm sure she was right. Certainly this has to be the source of the success of the fish finger that all children, including my own, devour.

# Rose

*R.D.* Rose is the mother of Michael, and Michael is the husband of Lucy, my youngest daughter. Rose is a pure-bred Cherokee Indian from the south-west of the United States, and this alone makes her a far more interesting and complex person than most of us Anglo-Saxons.

In middle age, Rose is alight with energy. It seems to spark out of her like something electric. She can look after herself in all circumstances and always has. She is inventive, original and has an unwavering artistic eye. You might guess, therefore, that when she was asked to provide a few recipes for our family cookbook she would come up with something pretty unusual and especially delicious. She has not let us down with this Paella Salad. Each one of her other remarkable contributions is also highly recommended, especially, for me, the Sweet Potato Pone (p. 178).

## *Paella Salad*

ROSE

Serves 6–8

$2\frac{1}{2}$ lb fresh or frozen squid, to reduce to about $\frac{1}{2}$ lb when cooked

about 1 pt milk

5 oz sugar-snap peas or mange-tout peas

5 oz cooked and peeled shrimps

10 oz shredded cooked chicken

2 oz diced celery

2 oz deseeded and diced green pepper

2 oz deseeded and diced red pepper

2 oz deseeded and diced yellow pepper

2 oz finely chopped onion (optional)

chopped parsley

salt and pepper, to taste

DRESSING

10 fl oz mayonnaise

5 fl oz sour cream

1 clove garlic, crushed

2–3 tsp very finely chopped ginger

1. Prepare the squid by pulling out the insides, which will be attached to the head. Pull out the plastic-looking quill from inside the body and any of the soft white material. Remove the purple-coloured skin from the body and fins. Cut off (above the eyes) the tentacles from the head and remove the beak-like mouth by squeezing the middle of the tentacles and discard.
2. Wash the body well inside and out.
3. Cut the body into rings $\frac{1}{4}$ in. thick and the tentacles into strips.
4. Place the squid in a large saucepan with just enough milk to cover them, cover with the lid and place over a moderate heat. After 2 minutes, remove the lid and give a good stir,

replace the lid and simmer about 3 minutes more. Eat a piece: it should be deliciously tender and rosy pink in colour. Strain and allow to cool.
5. Blanch the sugar-snap or mange-tout peas and refresh immediately.
6. Place the squid, sugar-snap or mange-tout peas and all the other ingredients together in a bowl and mix well.
7. Make the dressing by combining the ingredients and correct the seasoning. Pour over the salad and toss.

Serve with hot bread.

## *Spiv's Favourite Pasta Sauce*

A variation on the traditional Italian pesto sauce, using ingredients easily available all year round. It stores well in the refrigerator for 3–4 days if kept in a screw-top jar.

Serves 6

2 oz chopped fresh coriander leaves, stalks removed

3 oz hazelnuts, toasted and chopped so they still are crunchy

3 oz freshly grated Parmesan cheese

1 tsp salt

ground black pepper

4–5 tbsp olive or hazelnut oil

1. Mix together the coriander leaves, hazelnuts and Parmesan cheese.
2. Add salt and pepper.
3. Slowly add oil.
4. Heat gently in small saucepan, but do not allow to boil.
5. Mix into drained pasta and serve immediately.

Parsley can be substituted for coriander leaves but the sauce is less surprising.

## *Fran Collins's Pasta Sauce*

Serves 6

4 tbsp olive oil

4 cloves garlic

2 anchovies

2 × 14-oz cans tomatoes

1 tbsp capers

pinch dried chilli powder

10 black olives

10 green olives, chopped

5 oz grated Parmesan cheese

1. Heat the oil in a pan, fry the garlic until brown, then remove and discard garlic.
2. Add anchovies, chopped or pressed through a garlic press, and tomatoes to the oil. Cook gently for 30 minutes.
3. Add the rest of the ingredients and cook for a further 15 minutes.
4. Cook enough pasta for 6 servings.
5. Mix with the sauce.
6. Serve with the grated Parmesan cheese.

## *Moussaka-type Lasagne*

ASTA

Serves 6

4 oz butter

2–3 onions, coarsely chopped

1–2 cloves garlic

2 green or red peppers

8 oz mushrooms, sliced

14-oz can tomatoes

4 tsp sweet paprika

salt and pepper, to taste

1 lb cooked mince

1 tbsp oil

10 sheets dried green lasagne

1 pt béchamel sauce

8–12 oz grated Lancashire cheese

1. Heat 2 oz butter in a pan and gently fry the onion and garlic.
2. Add the peppers and cook another 5 minutes, adding the remaining butter if necessary.
3. Add the mushrooms, tomatoes, paprika, salt and pepper.
4. Add the meat and heat through.
5. Bring a pan of water to the boil, add salt and 1 tbsp oil and return to the boil. Add the lasagne and boil without a lid until *al dente*, about 10–15 minutes. Drain and separate.
6. Fill a deep ovenproof dish with alternating layers of meat mixture and lasagne. Top with béchamel sauce, cover with grated cheese and put under a slow grill till the cheese is crisp. Serve immediately or put in a low oven, about 225°F / 110°C / Gas mark $\frac{1}{4}$, to keep hot. It will be OK even 2 hours later.

Serve with spinach salad and many glasses of wine.

# *Quentin Blake*

*R.D.* What do you know about Quentin Blake? Not very much. But why is this? After all, here is a man who, to my mind, is the finest illustrator of children's books in the world today and whose work is known to millions in many countries, and yet only very few people know much about this charming, witty, gifted and rather shy artist.

I and most of my family are privileged to know him well and everyone adores him. He has illustrated with amazing flair fourteen of my children's books so far and it is Quent's pictures rather than my own written descriptions that have brought to life such characters as the BFG, Miss Trunchbull, Mr Twit and The Grand High Witch. It is the faces and the bodies he draws that are remembered by children all over the world.

And yet because Quent is essentially so modest and retiring, very few people even know what he looks like. He is somewhere in his fifties and although he is by no means plump, he gives the impression of being round rather than long. The top of his head is rather bald and under it is a cherubic face that gazes out upon the world with amused tolerance. When he and I work together on a new book and he has a pen in his hand, it is magical to watch the facility with which he can sketch out a character or a scene. 'You mean more like this?' he will say, and the nib will fly over the paper at incredible speed, making thin lines in black ink, and in thirty seconds he has produced a new picture. 'Perhaps,' I will say, 'he should have a more threatening look about him.' Once again the pen flies over the paper and there before you is exactly what you are after. But this is not to say that I 'help' him with many of the characters he draws for my books. Most of them he does entirely on his own and they are far better and funnier than anything I could think of.

Like all of us, Quent is a discerning pig where food is concerned. He even has a small house in France where he can eat *their* food on his doorstep.

When Liccy asked him for a recipe for this book, his immediate reply was the extraordinary 'Savoury Crocodile'. (This was clearly a reference to the very first book of mine that he illustrated, *The Enormous Crocodile*.) Who else would cook like this? Josie's brilliant interpretation can be seen in Jan's photograph of the Children's Party on p. 162, and it is typical of Quent that he came up with what was easily the most original recipe. The children loved it.

# SAVOURY CROCODILE

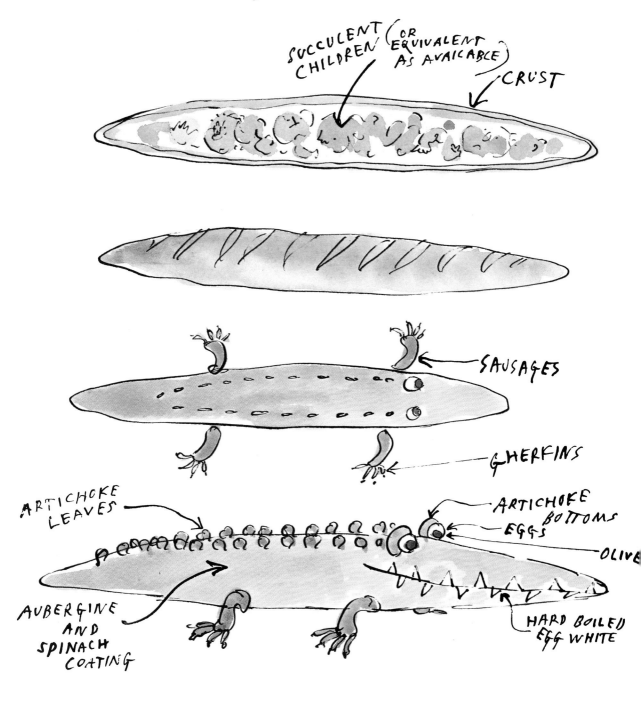

SUCCULENT CHILDREN (OR EQUIVALENT AS AVAILABLE)

CRUST

SAUSAGES

GHERKINS

ARTICHOKE LEAVES

ARTICHOKE BOTTOMS

EGGS

OLIVE

HARD BOILED EGG WHITE

AUBERGINE AND SPINACH COATING

# VEGETABLES AND SALADS

# Vegetables

*R.D.* These are surely the greatest of all foods, but unfortunately in order to appreciate them fully you have to grow them yourself. Only then can you obey the golden rules that govern the serving of perfect vegetables. The basics are as follows:

1. All vegetables (with the exception of main-crop potatoes) should be picked very small. The broad bean should be no larger than your little fingernail. The runner bean should be 5 or 6 inches long maximum, the carrot, very, very small and the leek as thin as an old-fashioned fountain pen. The same general rule applies to parsnips, turnips, beetroot and peas, Brussels sprouts and, of course, new potatoes.

2. No vegetables should be picked or dug until you are ready to

cook them. I realize this is impossible for the town dweller, but it really is the only way you will taste them in all their glory. You see, it is a curious but little-known fact that the moment a vegetable is plucked from its mother-plant, mysterious enzymes go to work to convert the sugar they contain into starch. The disappearance of sugar and the substitution of starch helps to preserve the picked vegetable and stop it rotting, but it doesn't help the flavour. This phenomenon is particularly noticeable in sweetcorn. Americans, who are very knowledgeable and particular about their sweetcorn, and grow a lot of it in their gardens, will seldom go out and pick the ears until the water is actually boiling in the pot. The same rule applies to virtually all the vegetable family.

3. All vegetables should, of course, be slightly undercooked so that texture is maintained and flavour preserved.

For me, the prince of them all is the young broad bean. A plateful of those, lightly painted with melted butter and sprinkled with a little salt, eaten all alone on a warm plate before the main course is the ultimate joy. There is nothing like it. The tenderness and the extraordinarily subtle flavour are indescribable. But never, absolutely never, adulterate the taste by putting them on the same plate as the meat and the gravy. The first picking of small young peas should be treated in the same way and they are very nearly, but not quite, as amazing. In fact, as the French know very well, all fine young vegetables should be eaten quite alone as a separate celebration.

I was once taken to lunch at the Savoy Grill by a famous theatrical producer. To the head waiter he said, 'Do you have any broad beans in yet?' 'Yes, sir,' replied the elegant flunkey, 'they've just arrived.' 'Then I'll have some,' said the producer, 'and peel them!' The head waiter turned white but kept his mouth shut.

Large broccoli spears, beloved by expensive restaurants, I find very dull and almost tasteless, hence they are invariably served with hollandaise to make them palatable. But the other kind, the purple-sprouting and the white-sprouting broccoli, are lovely crops to grow and will keep you supplied with tiny tender shoots for at least six weeks in early spring.

New potatoes, freshly dug and gathered small, are another very great delicacy, and I think that today the best one to grow is Sutton's Foremost. But don't ever let them get bigger than a greengage. I'm afraid all the imported new potatoes that come flooding into the country from Cyprus, Malta, Egypt and Israel before our own are ready have lain about far too long to have much flavour, but they are anyway a change from the old main crop of the winter and are, of course, a promise of better things to come.

I love the sweet potato and I cannot understand why more of them are not eaten by the British. They are far better for you than the ordinary starchy large potato because they contain incredible quantities of fibre and roughage. It should interest you to know that the consultant pathologist at the High Wycombe General Hospital once spoke to me as follows: 'There is a large population of West Indians in High Wycombe and their staple diet is sweet potatoes or yams. Because of the very high fibre content in these vegetables, I have never once in this hospital had a single instance of a black person suffering from any disease of the colon or the bowel. It is quite remarkable. Whereas these problems are virtually endemic among whites who do not eat this wonderful food.' So take note of that, all you eaters of baked white potatoes who believe they are so healthy. Try a baked sweet potato instead.

## Carrots with Cumin and Ginger
### VIRGINIA

Serves 4–5

1 lb carrots, if young leave whole, otherwise
cut into julienne strips
2 oz butter
½ oz brown sugar
½ tbsp white wine vinegar
1 tbsp cumin seeds
½ oz finely chopped fresh ginger
2 tbsp chopped parsley
salt and pepper

1. Steam or boil the carrots until just tender.

2. Meanwhile, place the butter with the brown sugar and vinegar in a saucepan and stir until everything has melted and combined.

3. Add cumin seeds and fresh ginger. Then toss with the freshly cooked carrots and parsley.

4. Season and place in serving dish.

This is one of my most favourite dishes. I do wish the English would eat their vegetables in the French manner, as a course on their own, tasting each delicate flavour.

## Marius's Carrots

Serves 4–5

1 oz butter

1 lb carrots, peeled and sliced

1 small onion, peeled and sliced thinly

2 tsp brown sugar

4 fl oz single cream

salt and pepper

chopped parsley

1. In a frying pan (preferably with a lid) melt the butter.
2. Make alternate layers of carrots and onions.
3. Cover and simmer very slowly until tender, about 20 minutes.
4. Season with salt and pepper and sprinkle over the sugar.
5. Pour in the cream and continue to cook for a further 10 minutes.

Place on a serving dish and sprinkle with the chopped parsley and serve.

## Cauliflower and Shrimps

ASTA

As a child the summer holidays in Norway were always the highlight of the year. The weather was always fine and Louis, my eldest step-brother, used to somehow make our ancient motorboat, *The Hard Black Stinker*, go, and we would go off to the islands picnicking and bathing, coming home to our hotel in the early evening. On nearing home we would always hear the chug-chug of the shrimp boats returning and we would hand up our buckets for the fresh cooked shrimps, which we peeled and ate on the spot. Ever since my favourite food has been shrimps, and my mother used to make this simple supper dish.

1 cauliflower, cooked whole

1 pt white sauce with 2 tbsp dry sherry

1 lb peeled shrimps

Mix shrimps into sauce and pour over cauliflower.

My own recipe for shrimps is:

Cut the pink flesh of some watermelon into cubes and remove the black seeds. Mix this with mayonnaise and a generous helping of shrimps. Serve very cold in glasses with plenty of brown bread and butter.

A very simple summer dessert from my Norwegian holiday was rips. These are redcurrants stripped from their stalks and covered with caster sugar. They are then coated in a real custard, made with thin cream in which a vanilla pod has been cooked. They are equally delicious served with cream.

As a child I always hated breakfast, and to keep me sitting in the hotel dining-room my mother would order two raw egg yolks in a long glass, add two tablespoons of caster sugar and tell me to keep beating them until they turned white. Then I could eat them – very good, known as Eggedosis, and even better with a little brandy added, but I never got that at breakfast.

This is not a recipe but an incident that happened during the war. I was home on leave from the WAAF and my mother was entertaining some very special guests to Sunday lunch. She had managed to get a rabbit and with her special magic, using bacon, carrots, onion and herbs, etc. had turned the dish into a feast. She asked me to carry it through to the dining-room, but at the kitchen door I tripped over the step and fell flat on my face, rabbit casserole and all. We scooped it up, put it in another dish, warmed it up, washed the floor; nobody was any the wiser and it still tasted delicious.

# *Three Sisters*

*R.D.* Although our parents were living here in Britain (actually in Wales) when we were born, they were still totally Norwegian, and almost no English was spoken in the house. It was therefore natural that we were all given Norwegian names: Alfhild, Roald, Else and Asta. Alfhild, known as Alf, is 76, I am 74, Else is 73 and Asta is 70, so you can see that we are all getting long in the tooth.

Alf, the eldest, was and still is a genuine eccentric. Her life has been eccentric right from her younger days. As a vivacious young girl in her early twenties she let fly among the clever and successful males of London, composers (William Walton), writers (Arthur Bryant) and all sorts of other interesting fellows. She smoked cigarettes and drank champagne out of her shoe and danced on table-tops and got out of bed late in the mornings. Then suddenly she married and changed her style completely. She married a man even more eccentric than she was, a small, not very prepossessing person who had no job and didn't want one, and the two of them holed up in a thatched cottage in a remote village in Buckinghamshire called Ludgershall, but still, note carefully, not many miles from our mother. They lived in great frugality on a tiny amount of capital, and their interests were in gardening and eighteenth-century architecture. Even with almost no money, the eccentricity manifested itself in their somehow managing to acquire a small, very beautiful second-hand Rolls-Royce coupé, complete with the number plate DOS 1, and in this they would cruise around the countryside, visiting and admiring fine old country houses and their gardens.

Neither of them ever worked at a paid job or earned any wages. Rather than work at earning money, which either of them could easily have done, they preferred to live in comparative poverty. It

*Asta, Else, Alf, Roald*

was an extraordinary way of living, and after her husband died, Alf and her one daughter still live in more or less the same way, in a small cottage in a small village. In the same village, a few hundred yards away, lives one of our sisters, Else, and a few miles further on is my own home. We all still keep in very close touch and see each other at least twice a week.

Else is the complete opposite of Alf. She has followed the pattern of her mother, marrying a man she loved, raising a family of three children and devoting herself totally to this end. There is no eccentricity here, just a calm cruise through a life where the children and grandchildren are everything and her task is to stick around and help them all she can. Her children and their husbands group themselves

*Alf, Asta, Roald, Else*

around her and love her dearly. An expert gardener, a great cook and nobody's fool, she has mastered the art of being a fine wife and mother and living a calm life.

Asta, the youngest, is not in any way like the other two. She was always the doer, the active one with endless energy. In the war she joined the women's branch of the RAF, the WAAF, and very soon became an officer, first in rather dangerous front-line radar stations on the south coast and then in barrage balloons, which ringed our cities and forced the German bombers to fly high. Towards the end of the war she went to Norway in command of the WAAF over there and I believe she earned a medal from the king of that country. But when she married a veterinary surgeon, she settled down (no more than five miles from the mother, of course) and devoted herself to her husband and her three children.

Asta is every bit as good a cook as her two sisters, but the one thing she excels in above all others is first the growing and then the preparing of her own vegetables for the table. In the right seasons her kitchen garden is a wonder to behold, with its serried rows of young peas and beans and carrots and beetroots and everything else you can think of, all carefully planted at intervals so that there is a continuous supply of young and tender crops.

## Asta's Carrots

Slice the carrots in rings and cook in water with at least 1 tsp of sugar until *al dente*. Strain into sieve, retaining the liquid.

Put 1 oz butter in a small pan, add ½ oz flour, mix and add liquid. Reduce to a thin cream. Add carrots and a good tbsp of parsley. Serve.

## Asta's Spinach

Very few people know how to cook spinach, whether they cook their own or buy frozen chopped spinach.

Squeeze out all the water. Melt 1–2 oz butter in a small saucepan. Add the spinach and stir around till mixed with the butter. Add 1–2 tsp sugar. Add salt and pepper and a grating of nutmeg. Then pour in cream and milk till the right consistency. Correct seasoning. Now, whatever you do, remove from the heat and heat up only a minute before serving. Otherwise it goes brown and horrible.

## Josie's Spinach

Serves 4–5

2 oz butter

1 onion, chopped

2 tbsp sesame seeds

2 lb spinach, stalks removed and leaves washed and dried

½ nutmeg, finely grated

6 tbsp single cream

lemon juice

salt and pepper

a little milk

1. Melt butter in a large frying pan.

2. Fry onions and sesame seeds until lightly browned.

3. Gradually add all the spinach, stir occasionally until the leaves are limp and cook for 2 minutes.

4. Place leaves in a food processor and chop roughly.

5. Add the nutmeg, cream, a little lemon juice, salt and pepper.

6. Return to frying pan and reheat.

7. Add a little milk if necessary, correct seasoning and serve.

# Charlotte

*R.D.* Charlotte is my second step-daughter. She is still a single career girl but I would take bets that she won't stay single for long: she is too attractive and family-loving for that. She is a successful freelance interior decorator who, with her taste and flair, can turn a shabby-looking little house or flat into a cosy palace. Any daughter of Liccy's was bound to become a superb cook and Charlotte's deft fingers can create wonderful dishes from the simplest ingredients.

## Charlotte's Parcels

Serves 6

12 oz fresh spinach

1 oz butter

1 shallot, thinly sliced

6 tomatoes

6 rashers smoked bacon

6 oz Gruyère cheese

14 fl oz *crème fraîche*

salt, pepper and freshly grated nutmeg

1 packet (10½ oz) filo pastry

4 oz butter, melted and clarified

6 tsp Dijon mustard

1. Stalk and wash the spinach leaves and dry.

2. Melt the butter in a large saucepan. Add the shallot and spinach, place on lid and steam, stirring occasionally, and sweat until limp.

3. Place in a bowl and allow to cool.

4. Skin tomatoes and cut into quarters, deseed and cut in half again.

5. Preheat the grill, remove the bacon rind and grill bacon until crispy. Place on kitchen paper towels and allow to cool.

6. Slice thinly or grate the Gruyère cheese and set aside.

7. Stir the *crème fraîche* into the spinach, mix well and season well with salt, pepper and nutmeg.

8. Preheat oven to 450°F / 230°C / Gas mark 8.

9. Unroll the sheets of filo pastry. Place 1 sheet on a lightly floured surface, brush with the butter and fold in half.

10. Spread 1 tsp mustard just above the middle of the centre, then a spoonful of the spinach, and some crispy bacon pieces with some tomato pieces topped with the Gruyère.

11. Fold over the top edge of filo, then the sides, brush with butter and roll over using the remaining flap of pastry to close the rectangular parcel.

12. Repeat this until all is used. The mixture will make 12 parcels.

13. Place on lightly floured baking tins and bake for 25–30 minutes until crispy golden brown.

Serve with a salad.

## Caramelized Sweet Potatoes

These are excellent with ham.

Serves 4–5

approximately 1½ lb sweet potatoes
approximately 1 oz butter
approximately 3 oz demerara sugar

1. Boil the potatoes in water until almost cooked.
2. Cut them in quarters lengthways.
3. Melt the butter in a frying pan.
4. Add the potatoes and sprinkle with the sugar, which, melting and mixing with the butter, forms a kind of caramel. Turn potatoes in order to coat evenly, forming a very crunchy crust. This will take about 5–7 minutes.

Place in a warmed dish and serve.

## Potato and Chicory Soufflé

ANNE

Serves 6

8 oz chicory
2 lb potatoes
2 oz butter
1 clove garlic, crushed
6 tbsp double cream
3 eggs, separated
salt and pepper

1. Grease a 4-pt soufflé dish with butter and place upside down in freezer or fridge.
2. Remove any damaged outer leaves of chicory. Halve lengthways and slice thinly.
3. Cook potatoes.
4. Preheat oven to 450°F / 230°C / Gas mark 8.

5. In a frying pan melt 1 oz butter, add garlic and chicory. Cook gently for 10 minutes.

6. Drain and mash potatoes.

7. Mix the chicory, cream, egg yolks and seasoning into the potatoes.

8. Beat egg whites until stiff. Fold into potato mix.

9. Place in the soufflé dish and rough the surface. Dot with remaining butter.

10. Bake for 35–40 minutes.

Serve immediately.

## Potato Cake

### MARWOOD YEATMAN

For this you need an all cast-iron 8-in. frying pan, one that does not stick. It must have a metal handle. Any main-crop potatoes are suitable, waxy or floury. (The quantity of potatoes and the size of the container can be varied.) The cleaner the fat – the lighter in colour – the better the cake. It is very pretty, and excellent with roast beef or lamb. The salt keeps the outside crisp.

Serves 6

3 lb potatoes, peeled and sliced as thinly as possible

goose, duck or chicken fat, rendered

salt

1. Place the pan on a moderate heat. Put in just enough fat to cover the bottom. Distribute a little round the sides.

2. Starting at the middle, arrange the slices of potato neatly in circles on the surface of the pan so they overlap. Do not leave any spaces. Build up the layers, frying the potatoes gently meanwhile. Finish off with 2 tbsp of fat.

3. Cover with greaseproof paper and bake for 1¼

hours at 350°F / 180°C / Gas mark 4, removing the paper for the last 20 minutes.

4. Cut round the edge of the potato cake; shake it loose. Drain off excess fat.

5. Turn the cake out carefully on to a large plate. Dust with salt and cut into slices.

## Liccy's Foolproof Crunchy Roast Potatoes

Prepare 1½–2 hours before serving.

1. Peel and boil potatoes for about 10 minutes until the outsides are soft but the insides are firm.

2. While potatoes are boiling, place some dripping in roasting pan and put in a hot oven (400–425°F / 200–220°C / Gas mark 6–7), until the dripping is sizzling.

3. Drain the potatoes and put straight into the sizzling dripping. Be careful with splashes.

4. Turn, baste, sprinkle with salt and replace in the oven, on the top shelf if possible. The oven, by this time, should be reduced to the correct temperature for the meat.

5. After 15 minutes take out, turn and baste again. Replace in the oven and leave them. It is imperative they are left in the oven until the serving time, about 1½–2 hours later.

## *Potatoes and Onions with Cream and Garlic*

MARWOOD YEATMAN

Serves 6–8

2 lb waxy potatoes

10 fl oz milk

10 fl oz cream

1 large onion, peeled and chopped

salt and white pepper, to taste

butter

1 clove garlic, peeled

1. Peel and slice the potatoes, not too thinly.

2. Put the potatoes in a saucepan with the milk, cream and onion. Season with the salt and pepper.

3. Cook gently for 10 minutes, stirring occasionally. Add a little more milk if necessary.

4. Butter an ovenproof dish and rub with the garlic. Place the potato mixture in it and bake in the oven for 1 hour at 350°F / 180°C / Gas mark 4.

Serve immediately.

## *Kathy's Potato Crisp*

These are an excellent alternative to roast potatoes.

Serves 6

2 lb potatoes

salt

8 oz clarified butter

1. Dry peel the potatoes. Do not put them in water, as starch is needed to keep the potato together to form a cake.

2. Cut the potatoes into julienne or grate them, then salt.

3. Heat the clarified butter in a large frying pan until very hot.

4. Add the potatoes to the heated pan all at once, using a spatula to flatten them out.

5. Fry for about 5–7 minutes or until crisp.

6. Then flip the potato cake over and fry for a further 5–7 minutes until crisp.

7. Drain cake on kitchen paper towels. It is necessary to serve on a large warmed serving plate.

To serve, cut into wedges. Alternatively, you could make individual cakes.

## *Turnips with Chives*

ALI

The younger and fresher the turnips the better, as this method preserves the flavour brilliantly.

Serves 4

1½ lb turnips approximately

4 oz butter

2–3 tbsp chopped chives

1. Peel and chop the turnips into small cubes.

2. Blanch in boiling water for 2–3 minutes.

3. In a frying pan melt the butter; be generous – the butter should cover the turnips.

4. Add the turnips and cook very gently for 5 minutes and serve in the buttery juices sprinkled with the chopped chives.

# *Neisha*

*R.D.* Neisha is my oldest step-daughter. Her mother called her
Neisha from the very beginning because in order to hasten her birth
Liccy swallowed the entire contents of a bottle of Milk of Magnesia,
and the name has stuck with her ever since. Neisha is married to Bill,
who is an American designer of motor cars in England, and Neisha
herself, make no mistake about this, is an exceptionally talented and
creative textile designer. The moment she got her diploma at the
Royal College of Art she was fought over by the big fabric manufacturers and interior decorators and she hasn't looked back since.
Her designs are startling, original and very beautiful; so is she, and so
is her cooking.

## Neisha's Baked Aubergines

This can be eaten as a light meal with salad, or as a vegetable accompaniment to a main course.

Serves 6

12 oz aubergines

salt

2 medium onions

3 cloves garlic

6–8 tbsp good-quality olive oil

2 × 14-oz cans tomatoes, drained and chopped

bunch of fresh basil leaves, chopped

pepper

1 tsp sugar

5 tbsp water

2 tbsp tomato purée

6 oz grated Gruyère cheese mixed with 2 oz grated Parmesan cheese

1. Slice aubergines into $\frac{1}{4}$-in. slices lengthways. Lay them out flat on a clean tea towel and sprinkle with salt. Leave them for 30 minutes. Pat dry, turn them over and repeat.

2. Preheat oven to 300°F / 150°C / Gas mark 2.

3. Chop the onions and crush 1 clove garlic and fry until soft in 2 tbsp oil.

4. Add tomatoes, chopped basil, salt and pepper, and simmer for 15 minutes.

5. Add sugar, water and tomato purée, and simmer for a further 30 minutes.

6. Heat the remaining olive oil and crushed garlic in the frying pan and brown the aubergine slices on both sides. Drain on kitchen paper towels.

7. Place a layer of aubergine in the bottom of a gratin dish, cover with a layer of tomato sauce and a sprinkling of cheese. Repeat this until all is used, ending with a layer of tomato sauce topped with cheese.

8. Bake in oven for 30 minutes until bubbling and lightly browned.

## Parsnip and Carrot Bake

CALLIE

Serves 8

6 oz butter

1$\frac{1}{4}$ lb parsnips, peeled and grated

12 oz carrots, peeled and grated

12 fl oz single cream

freshly ground black pepper

2 cloves garlic

3 oz fresh breadcrumbs

chopped parsley

1. Preheat oven to 400°F / 200°C / Gas mark 6.

2. Grease a large, shallow ovenproof dish.

3. Melt 4 oz of the butter in a large frying pan and stir in the grated vegetables and sweat them, stirring occasionally until they are almost cooked.

4. Season with freshly ground black pepper.

5. Place in the dish and pour in the cream.

6. In a clean frying pan melt the remaining butter and crush in the garlic cloves with the back of a fork. Remove when golden, stir in the breadcrumbs and fry, stirring constantly, until they are golden.

7. Drain on kitchen paper towels before sprinkling on top of the vegetables.

8. Bake for about 15–20 minutes until heated through.

9. Sprinkle with the chopped parsley and serve.

## *Caponata*

Serves 6

2 lb aubergines

8 oz finely chopped celery

2 fl oz oil

3 oz finely chopped onion

2 tbsp white wine vinegar

2 × 14 oz cans Italian plum tomatoes

2 tbsp tomato purée

2 tbsp capers

4 flat anchovy fillets drained and
pounded smooth

salt and pepper

2 tbsp pine nuts

1. Peel and cut aubergines into $\frac{1}{2}$-in. cubes, sprinkle with salt and leave for 30 minutes, then pat dry.
2. In a pan sauté celery in the oil for 10 minutes.
3. Add onion and cook for another 8–10 minutes. Remove from the pan.
4. Sauté aubergines in oil over high heat for 8 minutes or until slightly browned.
5. Return onion and celery to pan, stir in vinegar, tomatoes and tomato purée, capers and anchovies, salt and pepper. Bring to the boil, simmer and reduce for 15 minutes, uncovered.
6. Add pine nuts and serve.

## *Baked Marinated Courgettes*

This is delicious with the Salmon Fishcakes on page 92.

Serves 6

2 lb courgettes cut into $\frac{1}{4}$-in. slices

MARINADE

large bunch parsley

3 cloves garlic, peeled

large bunch fresh basil

1 tbsp fresh or 1 tsp dried thyme

$\frac{1}{2}$ tsp each salt and black pepper

4 fl oz virgin olive oil

TOPPING

12 oz Gruyère or Emmental cheese, grated

$1\frac{1}{2}$ oz grated Parmesan cheese

1. Place courgettes in a bowl.
2. Purée marinade ingredients and pour over vegetables. Toss to coat evenly. Marinate for 30 minutes at room temperature.
3. Preheat oven to 400°F / 200°C / Gas mark 6.
4. Transfer the vegetables to an ovenproof dish. Sprinkle with the cheese. Bake for 25 minutes. The vegetables should be just tender.
5. Place under the grill to glaze cheese if necessary and serve.

## Fried Haricots Verts

CALLIE

Serves 4

1 lb *haricots verts*
3 tbsp lard or butter
3 cloves garlic, crushed
$\frac{1}{2}$ tsp salt
4 fl oz water
1 tbsp soy sauce

1. Top and tail beans. Wash.
2. Heat fat in a pan and add crushed garlic. Stir for 2 minutes.
3. Pour in beans with salt and stir for 1 minute. Add water and cover tightly with lid.
4. Cook for 5 minutes until beans turn fresh green colour.
5. Take off cover and add soy sauce and stir for another 5 minutes. When water is almost evaporated, beans are cooked.

Spring greens lightly blanched and quickly fried in butter and chopped garlic are delicious too.

# Marwood Yeatman and Liccy's birthday dinner

*R.D.* I wanted Liccy to have a fine dinner party on her fiftieth birthday. To be more precise, Liccy herself wanted to have a fine dinner party to which all her old friends would be invited, as well, of course, as everyone in our respective vast families. No ordinary meal would do for such an occasion, and no ordinary chef should be allowed to prepare it. Lengthy discussions took place during which Liccy's youngest daughter, Loopy, a bit of an eccentric herself, announced that she was acquainted with the most unusual but brilliant cook in the land. His name, she said, was Marwood Yeatman, but Mr Yeatman, Loopy added, was very choosy indeed about whom he cooked for. She would, however, do her best to convince the great man that we were people with moderately discerning palates who knew the difference between béarnaise and hollandaise.

Famous chefs these days seem to court publicity as assiduously as pop stars, and most of them are entrenched in some wildly expensive restaurant which they own or part-own and from which they will sally forth occasionally to supervise a party for a millionaire or an ambassador if the price is right. Not so Marwood Yeatman. He lives, as it happens, in a simple cottage in the West Country and he does not run a restaurant. He came to see us and he turned out to be a charming man, who would, he said, be happy to make a dinner for Liccy's seventy guests provided he chose the food and procured it himself from his own sources. His fee? Well, he seemed embarrassed

## LICCY'S BIRTHDAY MENU

White fish from Brixham, cooked in butter

Breast of hen pheasant with
a sauce of wild mushrooms
picked by the cook in the New Forest
A very few leeks pulled this morning
Salsify and viper's grass (scorzonera)

A 40 lb. York Ham from the Vale of York
Laver in season from Barnstable
Potatoes
A red and green salad with lamcress, sorrel and
lamb's lettuce
Red, white and blue cheeses

Apple and pear tarts
Orange pancakes
A whipped syllabut
Clotted cream from Bideford Market
New Forest butter from Blissford
Melba Toast

Coffee and Smarties

even to discuss such a thing, but he assured us it would be reasonable. And by golly, it was.

We had never before met a person who took such immense care in selecting the ingredients for a meal and, in particular, the precise places those ingredients came from. For example, he wanted a York ham for our dinner, and in order to get what he considered was absolutely the best there was, he drove up to Yorkshire and selected his ham personally. How many would do that?

This was December and certain foods were in prime season. Marwood wanted fish that was absolutely fresh. He got it from a Brixham trawler man. He wanted breast of pheasant, but it must be hen pheasant and he saw to it that it had been hung exactly right to the day. He wanted wild mushrooms, so he used ones picked earlier in the season and dried at home. He knew all about mushrooms and where to find them and he gathered a basketful of several different varieties. He ordered thin leeks that must be pulled that day. He found salsify and viper's grass (scorzonera). He got laver (a kind of seaweed) from Barnstaple. 'This is the best time of year for laver,' he said. His red and green salad was made with landcress, sorrel and lamb's lettuce.

The cheeses were superb. Each had been collected by him from small dairies that he knew well, made with unpasteurized milk by expert and loving hands.

For the clotted cream, he went to Mrs Mills of Bideford's famous Pannier Market and for his butter to Mrs Sevier in the New Forest.

All this information I had to wring out of him in the kitchen while he was cooking on the afternoon of the dinner. 'Where is the menu?' I asked him.

'There is no written menu,' he said.

'In that case,' I said, 'would you mind if I wrote one out myself and had a copy made for each table? It would be a pity not to tell the guests about all these wonders you are preparing.'

Marwood agreed to this, and without pausing in his work, he went through a list of the foods we were going to eat. I had to keep pressing him for details. He did not, for example, volunteer the information that he had driven all the way up to Yorkshire for the ham. He divulged this, and indeed all the other details, only under close interrogation. So I wrote it all down. A copy of the menu is reproduced here.

The man is a wonder. He had a rather poky little kitchen to cook in, and he didn't arrive with the food until midday. He had one assistant, but he did nearly everything himself – for seventy people!

The food itself, when we came to eat it, was out of this world. I am not going to describe each item and how wonderful it tasted. But wonderful it all was, not least the tarts and the orange pancakes and the clotted cream that we had for dessert with our Sauterne.

Roald
and Liccy

Liccy and Jennifer

Callie

Phoebe

Michael and Lucy

Theo

Neisha

Lorina

Wendy

Ophelia

Anna

Roald and Charlotte

# *Laver*

## MARWOOD YEATMAN

Laver, the black butter (really dark green) of north Devon and Somerset, is the edible seaweed clinging to the rocks of the Bristol Channel in satin-like ribbons from Watchet to Hartland Point, and beyond. It is the laverbread of Wales, sloke in Northern Ireland, and *algue Celtique* to the French, which crops in the season for mussels and reaches perfection after the first frosts. A cool summer and calm sea produces a good harvest. In West Country people gathering laver can rouse the same instincts as beachcombing and, if taken from inaccessible places, requires the same set of tools: a rope, a bag and an extra pair of hands to haul pickings up the cliffs.

Fresh laver must be thoroughly washed in a stream, or underneath the cold tap, to remove the sand. Till late in the nineteenth century it was then cured in huts along the Devon and Somerset coast for pickling and powdering, or dried out in a bread oven overnight. Today the crop is boiled to a pulp for about four hours in water acidulated with vinegar or non-brewed condiment, and strained.

The sloke of County Down is often sold raw, with dulse, a close relation chewed like gum. In the established victuallers and market stalls of north Devon and south Wales, the laver is cooked, and comes loose. Steve the Fish in Barnstaple disposes of up to a quarter of a ton a week in winter. To see any at all away from the coast, even in tins, is unusual. A little laver used to go up to Marlborough with an Exeter man, also to Bath. The seaweed in London is likely to be imported.

The West Country pickers, some of whom are in their seventies and have eaten laver all their lives, swear by its iron content and say it purifies the blood. The flavour is unique: clean, pungent and improved with a little (bitter) orange juice. No salt or pepper is required. Laver is usually eaten hot as a sauce or a vegetable. It is not right with fish or beef, but good with fowls, lamb and pork; superb with bacon; and better with a hot ham than anything on earth. A couple of spoonfuls in soup can be fun too. In Northern Ireland laver is still served with some ceremony in a sloke pot.

## Braised Red Cabbage

ANNE

This is delicious served with pork or game.

Serves 8

2 lb red cabbage

salt and freshly ground black pepper

1 lb onions, thinly sliced

1 lb cooking apples, peeled, cored and thickly sliced

2 cloves garlic, finely sliced

3 tbsp brown sugar

2 tbsp caraway seeds

3 tbsp white wine vinegar

3–4 tbsp port or cider

1 oz butter

1. Preheat oven to 300°F / 150°C / Gas mark 2.

2. Discard tough outer leaves of cabbage, quarter, remove the hard stalk and then shred finely (slicing blade of a food processor is ideal).

3. In a large casserole (6-pt) place a layer of cabbage, seasoned with salt and pepper, then a layer of onion and apple with a sprinkling of garlic and sugar and caraway seeds. Continue to alternate these layers until all the ingredients are used up.

4. Pour in the wine vinegar and the port or cider, and dot with the butter.

5. Cover the casserole and let it cook very slowly in the oven for 3–3½ hours.

This dish will reheat successfully and therefore can be made in advance.

## Fried Cabbage with Bacon

### PRISCILLA

This is delicious with baked potatoes.

Serves 2–3

1 medium onion, chopped small
2 rashers streaky bacon, chopped
2 tbsp olive oil
1–2 cloves garlic, crushed
1 lb shredded green cabbage
salt and pepper, to taste

1. In a frying pan fry the onion and bacon in the olive oil for about 5 minutes.
2. Add the crushed garlic and cook for 2–3 minutes.
3. Now stir in the shredded cabbage (bulky at first but it will soon collapse).
4. Keep stirring so that it cooks evenly. The cabbage will take 10 minutes to cook *al dente*, a bit longer if you like it soft.
5. Season with the salt and pepper to taste.

## Cabbage in Cream

### ANNE

Serves 4

11 oz finely shredded white cabbage
5 fl oz *crème fraîche*
1 oz butter
1 tsp caraway seeds
salt and pepper, to taste

1. Blanch cabbage in plenty of boiling salted water for about 4–5 minutes. It should be very crisp. Refresh. Drain well and dry as much as possible.
2. Meanwhile, heat the *crème fraîche* with the caraway seeds.
3. Melt the butter and toss the cabbage in it so that each strand is coated, then pour in the cream.
4. Season with salt and pepper, and serve.

A far cry from school cabbage: even the most hardened, the most inveterate cabbage-hater will be converted.

# Theo

*R.D.* My son Theo loves to eat, but he is a typically male eater, with a good steak coming at the very top of his list. That, after all, is a sensible choice for someone who has a voracious appetite. But he is also curiously fastidious and will not touch certain foods. I doubt whether he has ever tasted a mushroom – he will carefully pick every tiny piece of mushroom out of a steak and kidney pie or any other dish. Nor will he allow one grain of rice to pass his lips. Yet he will swallow a raw oyster with relish. He is a qualified baker, but doesn't enjoy baking, and as far as cooking goes, he is strictly an eggs and bacon or grilled steak chef. So it is curious that he has chosen this delicious vegetarian recipe. Peanut lovers will adore it.

# Theo's Peanut Roast

Serves 4–6

8 oz whole shelled unsalted peanuts

4 tbsp sunflower oil

2 onions, chopped

4 large tomatoes, skinned, deseeded and chopped, *or* 1 oz sun-dried tomatoes, chopped small

2 small dessert apples, peeled, cored and diced

1 tbsp pine nuts

1 oz oatmeal

4 tsp fresh chopped sage

sea salt, pepper

1 egg

a little milk

1. Heat oven to 350°F / 180°C / Gas mark 4.
2. Grease a 1-lb loaf tin ($8 \times 4\frac{1}{2} \times 2\frac{1}{2}$ in.).
3. Chop, mince or grind the peanuts.
4. Heat the oil in a pan, add the onions, fresh tomatoes (but if using sun-dried do not add them at this stage) and apples and fry until softened.
5. Add the peanuts, pine nuts, oatmeal, sun-dried tomatoes, sage and salt and pepper to taste.
6. Bind with the egg and just enough milk to give a fairly moist consistency.
7. Press into the loaf tin and bake for 45–60 minutes.

Serve with a green vegetable or with a salad. Theo likes it with his steak!

# Wild Rice Risotto

JOSIE

Serves 4–6

2 oz wild rice

2 oz butter

1 onion, chopped

1 clove garlic, crushed

1 carrot, coarsely grated

1 courgette, coarsely grated

2 oz finely sliced mushrooms

7 oz long-grain brown rice, washed

5 fl oz dry white wine

15 fl oz light vegetable stock

1½ tsp ground coriander

1 tbsp lemon juice

1½ oz walnuts

knob of butter

salt and pepper, to taste

1. Add the wild rice to 10 fl oz boiling salted water, then simmer for 35–40 minutes, until chewy yet tender. Drain well.

2. Melt the butter in a pan, add the onion and garlic and cook for 5 minutes.

3. Add the carrot, courgette and mushrooms, and cook for 4 minutes.

4. Add the long-grain brown rice and stir well.

5. Pour over the wine and stock and simmer until they have been absorbed (about 30 minutes). Keep a check on the liquid, as the risotto needs to be moist. Stirring the rice will give the risotto a creamy texture.

6. Add the cooked wild rice and mix well.

7. Mix in the coriander, lemon juice, walnuts, knob of butter, and salt and pepper.

8. Press into a buttered mould. Leave for a few minutes before turning out and serving.

Serve this dish with a main course or on its own with a crisp green salad.

## Baked Fennel with Mousseline

Serves 6–8

3 lb fennel
1 oz butter
1½ tbsp chopped fresh mint
1½ tbsp chopped fresh parsley
juice of 1 lemon

SAUCE
5 egg yolks
6 oz butter
juice of half lemon
pinch of salt
5 fl oz whipping cream

1. Preheat oven to 350°F / 180°C / Gas mark 4.
2. Prepare the fennel by trimming off the shoots and a thin slice from the base of the bulb.
3. Remove any discoloured outside leaves and cut the bulb in half across the widest part.
4. Place in an ovenproof dish.
5. Melt the butter and add the chopped mint and parsley and lemon juice.
6. Pour over the fennel, cover with kitchen foil and bake in the oven a good 1½ hours or until tender.
7. Meanwhile, make the sauce. Heat the container of the food processor by filling with very hot water and letting it stand for 5 minutes.
8. While it is warming, heat the butter in a small pan until it foams, then add the lemon juice.
9. Drain food-processor container and dry with a cloth. Put in the egg yolks and process for 30 seconds, then pour the hot butter and lemon juice through the lid while continuing to process. Stop as soon as all is added.

The heat of the butter should be enough to cook the egg yolks, thus thickening the sauce very slightly. If this has not happened, pour the sauce into a bowl on top of a saucepan of simmering water and stir until it has thickened.

10. Taste, add salt and adjust if necessary with more lemon juice. Just before serving, whip the cream to ribbon stage and carefully fold into the sauce.

Pour into a sauceboat and serve immediately with the baked fennel.

## Ali's Ail (Ali's Roast Garlic)

This is delicious with lamb. Fresh garlic is best if you can get it; the cloves are larger and more juicy and when roasted the crunchy outside contrasts with a lovely fluffy inside.

If you are roasting a 'quick' joint, such as rack of lamb or fillet, the temperature will be good and high (425°F / 220°C / Gas mark 7) and the cloves can be sprinkled around the meat, basting in the juices a couple of times for the 30 minutes or so that it takes to cook. When the meat is cooked, put it to one side to rest and turn the heat up to 465°C / 240°C / Gas mark 9 for a short blast – 10 minutes or so – until the garlic is a lovely dark brown.

# Onion Rings and Fried Parsley

ONION RINGS

onions

seasoned flour

vegetable oil

salt

1. Peel the onions and cut into $\frac{1}{8}$-in.-thick slices, against the grain. Separate the rings.

2. Lightly dust them with the seasoned flour, shake off any surplus. (We do this inside a large polythene bag.)

3. Deep-fry in hot fat till crispy and golden.

4. Drain well and season with salt.

FRIED PARSLEY

vegetable oil

a large bunch of parsley, washed and dried thoroughly (you will need lots of parsley, as it shrinks considerably)

1. Heat the fat in a frying pan.

2. Place a few sprigs at a time in the fat, taking care because the fat bubbles and spits.

3. Fry for a few seconds, until a deep green, then take the parsley out, drain and serve.

*L.D.* If I look up someone in *Who's Who* the first thing I look for is their hobby. The reason for this is fairly obvious but often one is surprised. They can be pretentious, pompous, non-existent, unusual, fun but they will always tell you a little about the person. One of my husband's hobbies is mushrooming. He really loves it. Gumboots on, taking a basket, walking stick and Chopper – our Jack Russell, off he goes. We have a marvellous field above our orchard and early in the morning, hidden amongst the grass and cow-pats these little white jewels glitter. He has one problem: his bad back and hip-replacements make bending very difficult. But for a mushroom nothing is too difficult.

There is only one way to cook freshly picked wild mushrooms. It goes straight into the frying-pan with a little butter, from the frying-pan on to a hot piece of toast with the juices poured on top. Sprinkle with a little salt and eat immediately.

# Mr Wells

## ANN TWICKEL

Charles Wells was from one of the several families that emigrated from Buckland to Coughton when the former was sold. He was my father's (Liccy's grandfather's) batman in the First World War and was with him when my father was killed. My first recollection of him was as footman and subsequently butler at Coughton. He was reputed to be half gypsy and, having seen his mother and known him, I should say it was undoubtedly true. He used to cross canaries with goldfinches and the results were brindled birds that sang more loudly and penetratingly than any other. Ferreting for rats and rabbits, nightlines for eels and rook shooting (the latter resulting in rook pies much enjoyed by younger members of the family) were some of his many side lines. But he was a strict disciplinarian and had I misbehaved in his eyes he would refuse to serve me ginger beer at luncheon, which meant that everyone knew I was in disgrace. I also remember him once beating me with an egg whisk for making a nuisance of myself in the kitchen!

He was loved by all and his death left a gap never to be filled.

*Spiv and Mr Wells*

*Cucumber salad*

## Mr Wells's Cucumber Salad

This salad is perfect with cold wild salmon.

Serves 4–6

1 cucumber
generous sprinkling of salt
1 tbsp white wine vinegar
3 tbsp good-quality olive oil
salt and pepper

1. Peel the cucumber and slice extremely thinly.
2. Arrange in a circular pattern on a large flat plate. Do not make two layers.
3. Sprinkle generously with salt and leave to stand a good 30 minutes.
4. Drain off the excess water and pat dry.
5. Sprinkle the vinegar and oil over the cucumber and tilt the plate so it covers all the cucumber.
6. Season with pepper and a little salt. Leave to marinate for at least 30 minutes or so before serving. The cucumber must be translucent and moist.

## Mr Wells's Salad Dressing

This dressing must be made fresh each time.

1 tsp caster sugar
a couple of twists of salt and pepper
4 tsp white wine vinegar
4 tbsp olive oil
2 heaped tbsp fresh chopped mint
2 heaped tsp fresh chopped parsley

1. Mix the sugar, salt and pepper.
2. Add 2 tsp of the vinegar and stir.

3. Add all the olive oil gradually, stirring all the time.
4. Add remaining vinegar.
5. Lastly add mint and parsley. Leave to marinate for about 30–45 minutes.
6. To serve, place dressing in the bottom of a salad bowl.
7. Wash and dry a lettuce, place in the bowl and toss in the dressing.

## Mr Wells's Beetroot Salad

Mr Wells often prepared this dish of startling simplicity and even hardened beetroot haters succumbed. Wonderful with cold meat and baked potatoes.

If you are lucky enough to find yellow beetroot this dish made with red on one side of the plate and yellow on the other is very dramatic.

Serves 4–6

1 lb cooked fresh beetroot (*not* the vinegary sort)
2 tbsp white wine vinegar
2 tbsp white granulated sugar
1 tsp salt (coarse)
freshly ground black pepper
5 tbsp olive oil

At least 1 hour before it is to be eaten, using a mandolin slice the beetroot extremely thinly – as thin as tissue paper. Arrange in a circular pattern on a large flat plate. Do not make two layers. Sprinkle with the vinegar and then the sugar. Leave at room temperature for about three quarters of an hour to absorb flavours, not in the refrigerator. Half an hour before serving sprinkle with the salt, pepper and the oil and leave to marinate. If necessary add a little more oil before serving. It should be moist.

## Gipsy House Salad

GIPSY HOUSE VINAIGRETTE

Pommery mustard

1 clove garlic, bruised

pinch of sugar

balsamic vinegar

good-quality olive oil, such as Filippo Berio's
cold-pressed Extra Virgin Olive Oil

SALAD

A mixture of sunflower seeds, pumpkin seeds
and pine nuts

a carton of cress

a mixture of lettuces

1. Preheat oven to 375°F / 190°C / Gas mark 5.

2. Make vinaigrette by combining ingredients in the usual way and to your taste. We generally make a jar of this at a time.

3. Spread the nuts and seeds on a baking tray and place in the oven until golden brown. They will need to be turned occasionally to prevent burning.

4. Wash the cress and dry.

5. Wash the lettuces and shake or spin dry in a salad spinner. Take care not to bruise the lettuce.

6. Place lettuce in the salad bowl, sprinkle in the cress, seeds and nuts. Add vinaigrette and toss.

# *Dimity*

*R.D.* The friendships that Liccy made with other girls years and years ago all seem to endure in the most extraordinary way and even to grow closer. There is around her a whole circle of these old girl-friends, and when I say that the friendships are close, I really mean it. There is constant communication within this magic circle and there is no doubt at all that Liccy herself is at the centre of it, the everlasting adviser and helper in times of trouble. What I like about it is that they are all such lovely people.

Dimity is one of them. She and Liccy have known each other for over thirty years, and despite the fact that Dimity disappeared to Australia when she married, communications were never broken off. When we went to Australia in 1989 Liccy's first priority was to see 'my old friend Dimity', and the reunion was cataclysmic. Dimity lived with her husband in the bush outside Perth in a rather wonderful house that the two of them had built themselves; more than that, they had actually made each brick by hand in wooden boxes, using some crazy mixture of mud and clay in the old French Provençal style. Totally mad, but it worked and the house stood there as solid as a rock. The whole building was festooned with climbing plants and flowers and in the scrub all around there were kangaroos and wallabies hopping about.

Dimity, as you can see, is slightly dotty in a marvellous sort of way, and is a tremendous cook.

## *Dimity's Red and Green Pepper Salad*

A good way to skin the peppers is to char them in the charcoals of a barbecue. Alternatively, the peppers can be charred under the grill, but this will take longer.

Serves 6

3 red peppers
3 green peppers
good-quality olive oil
salt
a bunch of basil leaves, chopped

1. Place the whole peppers on the hot charcoals, turning until the skins are equally charred.
2. Place in polythene bags and tie them loosely. Leave for 10–15 minutes. The skins will easily shrivel and peel away.
3. Cut the peppers in half, remove the core and seeds.
4. Place on a serving plate, lightly coat with olive oil, sprinkle with salt and chopped basil. If possible, leave for a couple of hours to marinate before serving.

## *Special Tomato Salad*

### CALLIE

tomatoes

a little olive oil with several cloves of garlic crushed in it

a bunch of basil, chopped

salt and pepper

a little home-made mayonnaise, a little yoghurt, a little *crème fraîche*, mixed together to make enough to coat tomatoes

### GARNISH

chopped parsley

chopped chives

1. Slice the tomatoes thinly and lay in a circular pattern on a flat plate, overlapping the edges slightly, but do not make two layers.
2. Spoon over a little garlic-flavoured olive oil and sprinkle with the chopped basil, salt and pepper.
3. Leave to marinate at least 30 minutes before coating the top with the mayonnaise mixture.
4. Garnish with chopped chives and parsley.

Eat with large black olives, excellent salami and a hot baguette.

## *Lucy's Salad*

This is delicious with barbecued steaks.

Serves 4

4 fl oz vegetable oil

3 cloves garlic

5 slices bread, cubed

1 large cos lettuce

6 tbsp freshly grated Parmesan cheese

2 hard-boiled eggs, finely chopped

### DRESSING

4 anchovies; retain a few strips for garnish

4 tbsp extra virgin olive oil

juice of half lemon

2 cloves garlic

1 tsp Dijon mustard

$\frac{1}{2}$ tsp sugar

salt and pepper, to taste

1. Heat the vegetable oil in a frying pan. Place the 3 cloves of garlic in oil and smash with fork to release flavour. Remove garlic, and fry bread cubes until crisp. Drain on kitchen paper towel.
2. Wash and dry lettuce. *Break* into bite-size pieces.
3. Make the dressing by mashing the anchovies through a garlic press. Then mash the other 2 cloves of garlic through the garlic press. Add all other ingredients and combine thoroughly with fork.
4. Toss lettuce with the dressing and cheese. Sprinkle the finely chopped eggs and *croûtons* on top so they don't get lost during tossing, and garnish with anchovy strips.

# *Jennifer Neelands*

*L.D.* Jennifer is my oldest and closest friend. I have known her since we met as two little girls aged seven at a convent boarding-school just after the war. We have kept in close touch throughout the ensuing forty-five years, through all the turmoils of our early lives, and now through the more interesting but equally challenging period of middle age, and we are perhaps closer today than ever before. That is the main reason why Jennifer must be part of this book. The other reason is that although Jennifer always modestly denies being much of a cook, in fact she is a very fine one, producing the simplest of meals always with the highest-quality ingredients.

Here, instead of giving me a flamboyant recipe for some grand dish, she provides, in typical fashion, an unobtrusive recipe for salad dressing. This, in my opinion, is one of the hardest things to master. If she has a fault, it is that she leaves everything to the ninth hour, but it is worth waiting for.

## *Jennifer's Salad Dressing*

Sent on the nineteenth day of the ninth month of nineteen hundred and ninety at nearly nineteen hundred hours – in fact, a very long time after it was asked for!

$\frac{1}{4}$ tsp salt

1 clove garlic

2 tbsp olive oil

1. Put $\frac{1}{4}$ tsp fine salt into the bowl you are going to serve the salad in, preferably *not* a wooden bowl.
2. Cut 1 clove garlic in half. Remove the skin and the green centre, and with a dessert fork crush the garlic into the salt until you have a paste.
3. Add 2 tbsp olive oil and stir well, using the flat of the fork to make sure all the paste is off the bottom of the bowl. Fish out any remaining pieces of garlic using a fork as a sieve.
4. Add the salad, toss and turn when you serve but *not* before.

*Notes*

a. Much nicer with very fresh garlic.

b. The amount of salt really depends on the size of the cloves of garlic.

c. Use only olive oil. Obviously the flavour depends on the oil you use. I have found middle-price middle-pressing best.

d. Make sure any washed salad leaves are well dried.

# PUDDINGS

# *Puddings*

*L.D.* There is no question that if I had to cook professionally I would have a pudding shop. I adore making puddings and I adore eating puddings, whether they be steamed, boiled, fried, baked, iced or fresh.

At the age of about seven my parents took my sister Clare and me to Normandy. It was just after the war, my first trip abroad and my first experience of French cooking: rich Normandy food with all its butter, and thick cream to make those rich sauces. For my parents, who had suffered the war diet for so long, it must have been heaven; for a seven-year-old's half-starved stomach it was a great shock. I have only two memories: firstly, falling asleep drunk on Normandy cider under a large farmhouse table and, secondly, being constantly sick. No sooner had my feet touched the soil of Dover than I turned to my parents and said how delighted I was to be back and now we could have puddings and proper food. My parents despaired.

Josie, I know, feels the same way about puddings as I do. You have heard a fair bit about Josie earlier in this book. I would like to add my tribute. Her extraordinary talent, hard work and patience in compiling and testing the recipes have made this book possible. It was a mammoth task. We started the year together but owing to the sudden death of my youngest daughter, Lorina, followed by the serious illness of my husband, I naturally forgot all about the cookbook and Josie had to soldier on all by herself. She had never cooked for the camera before. We were offered a home economist but declined. We decided 'no cheating' and this rule was stuck to. With the photography we had only two reshoots and one of them you will read about later. Josie is a perfectionist, a quality that is essential in the great cook. I do not possess it, so again I thank her. The first recipe in the pudding section, Iced Pecan and Orange Mousse, is one of Josie's masterpieces and we all adore it. I hope you will too.

*Iced pecan and orange mousse*

# Iced Pecan and Orange Mousse

### JOSIE

Make in advance for freezing.

Serves 12

#### PRALINE

4 oz caster sugar

1 fl oz water

3 oz roasted, roughly chopped pecan nuts

#### MOUSSE

6 egg whites

9 oz caster sugar

7 fl oz double cream

10 fl oz single cream

1½ oz finely chopped candied orange peel

#### ORANGE-FLAVOURED CUSTARD CREAM SAUCE

1 pt milk

1 vanilla pod, split

6 egg yolks

4½ oz sugar

zest of 1 orange; use segments for decoration

#### CARAMELIZED ORANGE PEEL

2 oranges

2 oz sugar

1. Cover a baking tray with kitchen foil and lightly brush with oil.

2. Line a 4-pt terrine with cling film: dampening the sides with water helps to hold it in place. Alternatively, make a cone out of thick cardboard and line with greaseproof paper. Make sure you have enough space in your freezer to store it.

3. Make the Praline. In a saucepan bring to the boil the sugar with the water: *do not* stir. Leave until it turns caramel (golden brown).

4. Stir in the pecan nuts and pour the mixture on to the baking tray. Allow to go cold, then place in a polythene bag and lightly crush with a rolling pin.

5. Make the mousse. Begin whisking the egg whites, then gradually add the sugar. Place over a pan of simmering water and continue whisking until the sugar dissolves.

6. Remove from the heat and whisk until cold. The meringue will be very stiff.

7. Mix the double and single creams and whisk them until they thicken and form ribbons. Be extremely patient as this will take a very long time.

8. Fold the cream into the meringue mixture with the praline and the candied orange peel. Pour into the lined terrine and freeze for 8 hours at least or overnight.

9. For the sauce, place the milk with the split vanilla pod in a saucepan and bring to the boil. Meanwhile, place the yolks in a bowl with the sugar and whisk until pale and mousse-like.

10. Still whisking, pour on the milk until combined, then pour back into the saucepan. Over a low heat, stir continuously until the mixture thickens, to coat the back of a wooden spoon. Take care not to overheat the mixture or it will separate.

11. Pass through a sieve. Grate the zest of the oranges and whisk into the sauce until it's evenly dispersed.

12. Allow to cool, stirring occasionally to prevent a skin forming.

13. Make the caramelized orange peel. Using a potato peeler, remove strips of zest from the oranges.

14. Cut into very fine strands.

15. Place in a saucepan and cover with cold water, bring to the boil, drain and refresh.

16. Return the strands to the pan, add the sugar and just enough cold water to cover.

17. Place on heat, dissolve sugar, then boil until almost all the water has evaporated.

18. Drain in a sieve and leave to cool before using for decoration.

19. Lift the mousse out of the terrine by the cling film, then remove and discard the latter.

Decorate with orange segments and/or caramelized orange peel. Serve the mousse in slices with the orange-flavoured custard cream sauce.

# Krokaan

*R.D.* Everybody in Norway knows what *krokaan* is. They love it and they eat it in all sorts of sweet foods, but above all they eat it in ice cream. Over here, curiously enough, we have no such thing and if occasionally it is made by some enterprising cook, there is still no English name for it. I find this astonishing, because it is so delicious. As you will see from the recipe given below, it is simply a kind of crispy, crunchy toffee made from butter, sugar and almonds, and quite apart from the fact that its taste is so beguiling, it makes a most satisfying crunchy noise when you chew it. Ice cream, whatever flavour it is, is invariably a soft and silent meal, but when you fill it with *krokaan* chips, as the Norwegians love to do, it suddenly becomes something that goes *crunch* when you chew it instead of just floating silently down your throat. Not only that, but the glorious slightly burnt toffee flavour it imparts to the ice cream is irresistible. You *must* make it and, for my taste, the more *krokaan* you put into your ice cream, the better it is.

## Krokaan Ice Cream

Serves 10

KROKAAN
1 oz butter
2½ oz sweet almonds, skinned and coarsely chopped
¼ oz bitter almonds, skinned and finely chopped (see *Kransekake* recipe, p. 174); if unavailable, use sweet almonds
5 oz sugar

CRÈME ANGLAISE
1¾ pt milk
1 vanilla pod, split
10 egg yolks
9 oz caster sugar
4 fl oz double cream

1. Make the *krokaan* first. Lightly grease a piece of kitchen foil placed on a baking tray.

2. Mix the butter, almonds and sugar in a heavy frying pan.

3. Place over a moderate heat, stir all the time, taking care that it doesn't burn.

4. When it's a good golden colour, turn on to the greased kitchen foil.

5. Allow to cool completely.

6. Place in polythene bag and lightly crush into small pieces with a rolling pin.

7. Now make the *crème anglaise*. Place the milk and the split vanilla pod in a saucepan and bring up to the boil.

8. Meanwhile, place the yolks in a bowl with the sugar and whisk until pale and mousse-like.

9. Still whisking, pour on the milk until combined.

10. Pour the mixture back into the saucepan and, over a low heat, stir continuously until the mixture thickens to coat the back of a wooden spoon. (Be careful not to overheat the mixture or it will separate.)

11. Pass through a fine (or conical) sieve and allow to cool, stirring occasionally to prevent a skin forming.

12. When the *crème anglaise* has cooled, add the cream and pour into the ice-cream machine. Churn until almost frozen, then add the *krokaan* and churn for a further few minutes. Alternatively, pour into ice-trays, place in the freezer and churn frequently.

Either serve the ice cream straight from the machine or place it in a chilled container and freeze until required.

## Rose Petal Sorbet

### ANNA CORRIE

This is not actually my recipe, although I have adapted it. I have never seen it in any cookery book; it was given to me by a friend called Pat Shears, who has given me her permission to use it. I am most indebted to her. I have used it many times.

When I first made this recipe, I wandered around my garden smelling and tasting rose petals. You go for colour, taste and smell. Generally, those roses that smell sweetly usually have the best taste – sometimes they are pale coloured or yellow. I discovered you can use any colour rose, as long as at least half are pink or red. For flavour, I find that New Dawn is good (and prolific) and all my old-fashioned roses are wonderful; for colour, I use Rose Rugosa (also prolific). You need only the petals, in good condition, from a full blown rose at the height of its scentedness.

I like magic in cooking, and this recipe is magic. Nobody ever knows what the sorbet is flavoured with unless they are told, since the idea of eating rose petals does not immediately spring to mind. But it tastes as roses smell and it has a most amazing, entirely natural, colour.

Serves 4–6

1 pt water

8 oz sugar

zest and juice of 1 lemon

4 large handfuls scented rose petals

2 tsp glycerine

Dissolve the sugar in the water and boil hard for a few minutes to make the syrup. Remove from the heat and add the lemon zest and rose petals, pushing them down with a potato masher. At this stage the petals go a ghastly greenish-white or faded bluish-pink, depending on their original colour. The syrup goes the colour of weak tea.

*Rose petal sorbet*

Leave overnight in a cool place. Next day, drain this mixture through a colander lined with a clean drying-up cloth. You are now left with an unattractive bowl of what looks like wine dregs. Now the magic. First add the glycerine and then the lemon juice. Stir. Instantly the infusion becomes a brilliant puce pink and you are ready to freeze your sorbet. Stir regularly to prevent crystals forming.

Serve with home-made Langues du Chat or Crêpes Dentelles.

5. Slice the cake, and butter generously. Cut into cubes and cover the fruit with the cake, butter side up. Brown slightly under the grill.

6. Whisk the egg whites until they begin to stiffen. Continue whisking, adding the caster sugar approximately 1 tbsp at a time, until you have about 6 oz sugar left. Fold in the remainder with a metal spoon and pile on to the fruit and cake, peaking the meringue with a fork.

7. Bake in the oven for about 25 minutes or until the meringue has set.

Serve hot or cold with pouring cream.

## Heaven on Earth

### PIP

Serves 8

6 large cooking apples

juice of half lemon

2 oz sugar

4 ripe pears

2 tsp mixed spice

grated rind and juice of 1 lemon

1 Madeira or similar sponge cake

butter

6 egg whites

12 oz caster sugar

1. Preheat oven to 375°F / 190°C / Gas mark 5.

2. Peel, core and quarter the apples. Place in an ovenproof dish, add lemon juice and grated rind, and sprinkle the sugar over the apples. Cover the apples with buttered greaseproof paper. Bake until the apples soften but before they begin to break up (about 35 minutes).

3. Turn oven down to 275°F/140°C/Gas mark 1.

4. Peel and quarter the pears. Add them to the dish with the apples. Add the lemon rind and juice, and spice. Mix together gently.

## Spiced Pears in Cider

### DELIA SMITH

6 large firm pears

1 pt dry cider

4 oz sugar

1 vanilla pod, split

2 whole cinnamon sticks

1 level dessert spoon arrowroot

some toasted flaked almonds

15 fl oz double cream, whipped

1. Preheat oven to 250°F / 130°C / Gas mark $\frac{1}{2}$.

2. Peel the pears neatly, leaving the stalks on, and stand them in a large casserole.

3. In a saucepan bring the cider, sugar, split vanilla pod and cinnamon sticks to the boil.

4. Pour this over the pears, cover the casserole and bake very slowly for about 3 hours, turning the pears half-way through the cooking time.

5. When the pears are cooked, transfer them to a serving bowl and cool.

6. Pour the liquid into a saucepan, discarding the vanilla pod and cinnamon sticks.

7. Mix the arrowroot with a little cold water to a smooth paste, then add to the saucepan with the liquid.

8. Bring to the boil, stirring till the mixture has thickened slightly to a syrup.

9. Pour it over the pears, allow to cool a little, then baste each pear with a good coating of the syrup.

10. Place in the refrigerator to chill thoroughly and serve sprinkled with toasted flaked almonds and whipped cream.

# Sophie

*R.D.* Sophie is my eldest grandchild. She is also the eldest daughter of Tessa, who is, in turn, my own eldest daughter. The brave little heroine of my book *The BFG* was called Sophie after the real one and Quentin's illustration below is based on her. That is the only time I have used a family name in any of my twenty-odd children's books.

## Sophie's Lemon Mousse

Serves 4–6

1½ tsp unflavoured gelatin
juice of 3 lemons
grated zest of 1 lemon
3 large eggs, separated
5 oz caster sugar
pinch salt
10 fl oz double cream

DECORATION
chocolate leaves or fresh mint

1. Dissolve the gelatin with the lemon juice in a bowl over simmering water.
2. Beat egg yolks with half the caster sugar to the ribbon stage.
3. Fold the gelatin mixture and zest into yolk mixture.
4. Add pinch of salt to egg whites and beat to soft peak stage. Add remaining caster sugar and beat back to soft peak stage.
5. Without washing the beaters or whisk, whip cream until semi-stiff.
6. Fold 1 tbsp of egg whites into the almost set lemon mixture.
7. Fold cream and remaining egg whites into the mixture.
8. Pour into ramekins or a single soufflé dish.
9. Chill for several hours.
10. Decorate with some chocolate leaves or with sprigs of mint and serve.

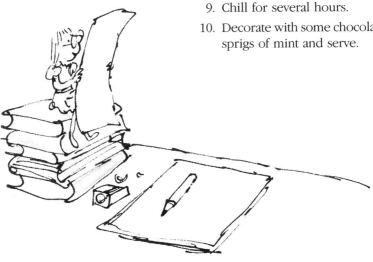

# Hot-house Eggs and Olivanas

*R.D.* I have no time at all for those husbands who declare, usually with a kind of chauvinistic pride, that they can't even boil an egg. The implication here is that the wife's place is in the kitchen and it is her job to serve the master. I am not saying that husbands should necessarily be excellent cooks, but I do believe strongly that they should all be moderately competent. They should certainly be able to provide a decent meal for the family when the wife is tired or unwell, or when she might be in hospital having another baby. Even when none of these circumstances applies, it is nice to give her a break now and again. No music is more dulcet in a wife's ears than the words of a competent husband-cook saying, 'You stay where you are, darling. I'm going to do the supper tonight.'

When the husband cooks for the children, the best and easiest way is to give them the foods they love or, better still, a slight variation of something they love, a little surprise. Even the simplest of surprises will amuse them when they are very young. For example, I knew that my own children adored fried eggs and fried bread. Who doesn't? So one evening, in an effort to vary it a little, I first cut a hole about the size of an egg yolk in the centre of the slice of bread. Then I fried the bread on both sides, and I also fried the cut-out bit, the roundel. Just before the bread was fully fried, I cracked the egg and dropped it into the hole in the bread. The egg white spilled over very slightly on to the bread, thus fixing the egg in the hole. I flipped the whole thing over to give the egg a few seconds on the other side, and then served it on the plate with the fried roundel of bread separate, telling the child-customer that it was up to him or her to slip the roundel under the egg if desired or to plonk it on top of the yolk. Nothing could be simpler or sillier than this recipe, but for some mysterious reason children love it. We always called it Hot-house Eggs, don't ask me why.

Another even simpler spellbinder for the young was the dish my mother used to give us years ago and which I have copied many times ever since. You mash a banana on a plate. Then you mash into it a few drops of good olive oil. It is simply delicious. The olive oil seems to heighten the flavour of the banana and makes the whole thing into a gorgeous, smooth, soft, syrupy paste. The ultimate luxury is to have it with thick cream. We called this one Olivanas.

Anything that floats in the middle of a jelly is also appreciated, I suppose because it looks as though it's swimming. For floaters in jelly I've used Jelly Babies or Maltesers or anything else that comes to hand. The trick is, of course, to suspend these objects in the middle of the jelly and not let them sink to the bottom before the jelly is set, but if you know how to make Oeufs en Gelée (p. 54), which you should, then you will know how to do it. I once caused howls of delight by the childish device of mixing a quantity of those tiny things called Hundreds and Thousands all through the jelly just before it started to set. This gave it a slightly crunchy texture.

We also used to make a lovely sauce for vanilla ice cream with melted Mars Bars, but I expect you know all about that one.

Which reminds me, there was also the Creamy Kit Kat Pudding. This one will make any child in the world love you. Put a layer of Kit Kats in the bottom of the dish. Then a layer of whipped cream. Then a layer of Kit Kats. Then another of whipped cream and so on for as long as you like. Put the whole thing in the deep-freeze. Serve in slices when frozen. Yum-yum.

Then there was peanut butter on toast, crispy bacon and lots of mustard and cress on top. Don't ask me why children love these particular curiosities. The fact remains that they do, and that's that.

Chop up a couple of Crunchie Bars and mix them into a bowl of whipped cream. Freeze for an hour. Yum-yum again.

And now I must get all these disgusting tastes out of our mouths by finishing with the simple savoury that all children adore. It is simply a buttered egg baked in a small, round oven dish with a slice of almost any meaty thing underneath, pâté or ham or whatever. They love it.

None of this has anything to do with good cooking, although I do think you will find that an Olivana, if you haven't tried it before, is worth tasting yourself.

## A la Daube

### ELSE

While we were staying at a seaside hotel on the Oslo Fjord a famous Norwegian cook came to give a demonstration. We were all invited to sample what she had made, which was fruit in jelly. There was a big table in the garden under the apple trees full of colourful and decorative jellies served with whipped cream, and we made pigs of ourselves.

The cook was such a funny sight, short and bossy and round as a plum-pudding, with little black boot-button eyes. She always wore a white overall and a tall white chef's hat. After the demonstration she happened to notice that we

had a canoe and insisted on being photographed in it. We held it steady while she got in. She was holding the paddle aloft and beaming for the camera when the canoe capsized and she came up spluttering and very cross, shaking like one of her own jellies, with her chef's hat floating beside her, while we sniggered in the background!

Find yourself an interesting jelly mould that will hold at least 3 pt. Choose three contrasting jelly colours. Use jellies that are made from natural fruit juices and colours. Choose your fruits.

Canned fruit works better than fresh because of the different pectin and acid contents in the fresh fruit, which can affect the setting of the jellies. Decide which jelly you would like to be the base of the mould (when inverted it will be the top colour) and then the order of the remaining colours. Follow the jelly instructions for making, but don't use as much liquid because a firmer jelly is needed.

1. Make the first jelly. Pour a small amount of jelly into the mould. When it is at the point of setting, decorate it with some drained fruit.

2. Allow the jelly to set completely before adding the remaining jelly, taking care not to disturb the set fruit.

3. Allow to set completely before you start the next colour.

4. Follow the method as before with the other colour jellies and fruit until you've filled your mould.

5. It is very important to allow each colour jelly to set before adding your next colour so that it does not break the surface of the previous colour and mix.

To serve, dip the mould in hot water for a few seconds, remove, then place the serving plate on top and upturn. Gently shake to release the jelly and carefully remove the mould.

Serve with lightly whipped cream.

# *Chocolate*

*R.D.* My passion for chocolate did not really begin until I was fourteen or fifteen years old, and there was a good reason for this. Today chocolate-guzzling begins when the child is about five and it goes on with increasing intensity until the guzzler gets to be about twelve. After that, with the advent of puberty and the approach of adulthood, there is a gradual decline in consumption.

Things were different when I was young. The reason that neither I nor any of my generation developed the chocolate-guzzling bug early on was quite simply that in those days there were very few delicious chocolate bars available in the sweet-shops to tempt us. That's why they were called sweet-shops and not chocolate-shops. Had I been born ten years later, it would have been another story, but, unfortunately for me, I grew up in the 1920s and the great golden years of the chocolate revolution had not yet begun.

When I was young, a small child going into the sweet-shop clutching his sixpence pocket-money would be offered very little choice in the way of chocolate bars as we know them today. There was the Cadbury's Bournville Bar and the Dairy Milk Bar. There was the Dairy Milk Flake (the only great invention so far) and the Whipped-cream Walnut, and there were also four different flavours of chocolate-coated Marshmallow Bar (vanilla, coffee, rose and lemon). This was meagre pickings when you compare it with the splendid array of different chocolate bars that you see on display today.

Consequently, in those days we small boys and girls were much more inclined to spend our money either on sweets and toffees or on some of the many very cheap and fairly disgusting things that lay about in open cardboard boxes all over the shop. There were sherbet-suckers and gobstoppers and liquorice bootlaces and aniseed balls and all the rest of them, and we did not mind that the liquorice was made from rat's blood and the sherbet from sawdust. They were cheap and to us they tasted good. So on the whole, we made do with eating sweets and toffees and junk instead of chocolate.

Then came the revolution and the entire world of chocolate was suddenly turned upside-down in the space of seven glorious years, between 1930 and 1937. Here is a very brief summary of what happened.

1876   Chocolate was first used by the Spaniards, Italians and French in the early seventeenth century, but only as a drink. Then over 100 years later, in 1876, a Swiss chap called Peters mixed chocolate powder with sugar and condensed milk and made a solid chocolate bar. Thus chocolate as we know it was invented.

1905    Now, Cadbury's got into the act and began production of milk-bars, starting with the Dairy Milk Bar. That came first.

1910    The plain one, the Bournville Bar, came five years later.

1920    Then came the first great speciality chocolate bar, the Dairy Milk Flake. This was a milestone, the first time any manufacturer had started seriously playing around with chocolate in their Inventing Rooms.

1921 The following year the Cadbury's Fruit and Nut bar appeared on the market.

There was a pause of nine years after that, until 1930, when the revolution began. From 1930 to 1937 virtually all the great classic chocolate bars as we know them today were invented, and now, sixty years later, they are all still on the bestseller list. Here is how it went:

1930    Frys invented the Crunchie.

1932    Suddenly, a new company appeared – Mars. What had happened was this. Over in Chicago a man whose name actually *was* Mr Mars owned a small factory that had been making the Milky Way for a number of years. In fact, he had invented it himself and was doing pretty well with it. When his young son, whose name was Forrest, Forrest Mars, had finished his education as an industrial engineer at Yale University, his dad said to him, 'Son, there ain't room for two of us in this little business of mine.' He gave him $5,000 and the recipe for the Milky Way. 'Go abroad, my boy,' he said, 'and start your own business.'

So the young Forrest went to England, to the town of Slough, and in a small laboratory he started experimenting with the Milky Way to make it better. He wanted to make what he called a Chew Bar, a thing that had never been done before. He placed a strip of soft caramel on top of the Milky Way and then coated it with chocolate. But it is not easy to make chocolate stick to caramel, as Cadbury's discovered when, some time later, they made the Curly Whirly. Their chocolate kept flaking off the caramel. Parents complained that it went all over the carpet, and Curly Whirlies were withdrawn. But Forrest Mars already had the secret to this, and the Mars Bar was born. It swept the world, the first-ever Chew Bar. And very soon 600 million of them were being eaten every year in

England alone. That is ten a year for every person in the country. So if you didn't eat your ten bars last year, someone else was eating them for you.

1933 Black Magic appeared in boxes, and for some reason it is still a bestseller.

1934 Tiffin and Caramello appeared in the shops.

1935 The lovely Aero was introduced.

1936 Don't forget Forrest Mars. In spite of the phenomenal success of his Mars Bar, this genius was still experimenting in his laboratory down in Slough. What he had done was to take a little pea-sized pellet of dough flavoured with malted milk and explode it inside a vacuum. Then he coated the result with sweet milk chocolate, and hey presto, yet another classic beauty was born! At first Mr Mars called it by the charming name of Energy Balls, but this made the public smile, so he changed the name to Maltesers.

(Note: At the time of writing, Forrest Mars is still very much alive, although he refuses to reveal his age. The business he and his family run is extraordinary. Although it is now enormous, it has remained a family-run concern, so that Mr Mars is not answerable to any stockholders. He is therefore free to run things as he likes, and the way he likes is to treat his employees as one great happy family. Everyone shares in the profits. The employees can actually get a rise in salary every four weeks provided sales have gone up over that period. I have visited the factory and can testify that it really is run as one big happy family. So hats off to Mr Mars.)

In the year of the Malteser, Quality Street was also put on the market.

1937 This was another golden year during which monumental classic lines were invented: Kit Kats, Rolo and Smarties. 300,000 Smarties are eaten every minute. 10,000 million are gobbled up every year in the United Kingdom alone. This figure includes the eight a day (four after lunch and four after supper) that our dog Chopper consumes.

So there you have it. In the seven years of this glorious and golden decade, all the great classic chocolates were invented: the Crunchie, the Whole-Nut Bar, the Mars Bar, the Black Magic Assortment, Tiffin, Caramello, Aero, Malteser, Quality Street Assortment, Kit Kat, Rolo and Smarties.

In music the equivalent would be the golden age when compositions by Bach and Mozart and Beethoven were given to us.

In painting it was the equivalent of the Renaissance in Italian art and the advent of the Impressionists towards the end of the nineteenth century.

In literature it was Tolstoy and Balzac and Dickens.

I tell you, there has been nothing like it in the history of chocolate and there never will be. Ever since then the giant chocolate companies have been exhorting their inventors to come up with another bestseller as great as the Kit Kat or the Mars Bar, but they have not succeeded. We are no more likely to see another Crunchie or another Aero than we are to see another Mozart or Beethoven. So we must relish what we have and be grateful for it.

The dates themselves should be taught in school to every child. Never mind about 1066 William the Conqueror, 1087 William the Second. Such things are not going to affect one's life. But 1932 the Mars Bar and 1936 Maltesers, and 1937 the Kit Kat – these dates are milestones in history and should be seared into the memory of every child in the country. If I were a headmaster, I would get rid of the history teacher and get a chocolate teacher instead and my pupils would study a subject that affected all of them.

The children would learn from their chocolate teacher that over the past forty years there have been frantic efforts in the Inventing Rooms of the big chocolate factories to develop bestsellers that are as good as the great classic bars of the 1930s.

Up in York Rowntree Mackintosh developed the Mint Cracknell. They thought they had a winner. They didn't. The great sweet-eating public, meaning you, gave it the thumbs down.

Then Cadbury's, after an enormous amount of market research, found out that what the public liked was not a sharp minty or sugary flavour, but something bland, almost tasteless; the blander, the better. They learned this by studying the success of Heinz Baked Beans, which sell by the millions but taste of almost nothing at all. So they invented a bland, tasteless bar, which was actually two bars, one with a bland soft layer of nougatine, the other with an equally bland layer of cereal. They called it the Double Decker and it did pretty well. In its first year, 1978, they sold over 160 million Double Deckers.

But this was nothing compared with the sales of the blandest and most disgusting thing of all, the Creme Easter Egg. Every year, between Christmas and Easter, Cadbury's sell 200 million of these revolting fondant-filled horrors, easily the sickliest thing you can buy for about 20p. I won't eat them. Nobody I know eats them. But somebody is eating them, bucketfuls of them, there is no doubt about that.

The most luxurious chocolate makers in the world are

Fortnum and Mason in Piccadilly. On their fifth floor the air is redolent with delicious smells and everything is done by hand. Fondant centres are blobbed by hand into soft holes pressed into trays of loose starch, allowing a natural set of twenty-four hours. (The big companies use rubber moulds in which the fondant sets in a few minutes.) Peppermint centres are made from precious drops from numbered bottles of Mitchum Mint, the finest mint oil in the world, double-distilled and matured for four years. Each year they import thirty 224-lb barrels of Chun-chun stem ginger from China, and 500 lb of morello cherries sit in oak barrels of brandy for a full year before use. The chocolates are all dipped by hand. The clever invention used by the big companies is not allowed. It is a machine called the Keuter Enrober and it can dip chocolates at an enormous speed, but not so beautifully as Fortnum's do it by hand.

Expensive Bendicks chocolates and expensive Harrods chocolates and not quite so expensive Marks & Spencer chocolates are all made in the same factory, on a trading estate between the M3 and Winchester. Next door is a slaughterhouse, where a lonely ram can always be seen standing outside inviting sheep to the slaughter. Harrods won't thank me for telling you any of this.

But your chocolate teacher would tell it to you and very much more besides, and if I wasn't over-age, I would apply for the job myself.

Curiously enough, I myself am not fond of chocolate-flavoured foods like chocolate cake and chocolate ice cream. I prefer my chocolate either straight and pure or in the form of lovely bars like Kit Kat, Aero and Crunchie. I also adore so-called truffles if they are very light and dry inside, as Prestat makes them. But most people do adore chocolate cake and chocolate puddings, and that is why there are chocolate puddings, or, rather, chocolate desserts, in this book. I have eaten this particular one many times and I have to admit that it is quite extraordinary. It is so rich and concentrated that you get the feeling that you are eating about fifty large bars of pure chocolate with each spoonful. So don't eat too much of it, especially if you combine it with thick cream. Children are mad about it.

*Chocolate St Emilion*

## Chocolate St Emilion

Use the best-quality chocolate you can find.

Serves 8

8 oz Amaretti, crushed
2–3 fl oz Cointreau
1 lb Menier chocolate
4 oz butter
2 egg yolks
1 pt double cream

DECORATION
icing sugar

1. Soak the crushed Amaretti in the Cointreau.
2. Melt the chocolate in a *bain-marie*.
3. Remove from the heat and gradually beat in butter and egg yolks. Leave the mixture to cool.
4. Whip the cream until semi-stiff.
5. Gently fold the cream into the chocolate mixture.
6. Place in a lightly greased cake tin (8-in. diameter × 2½-in. deep) alternate layers of chocolate mixture and Amaretti.
7. Chill for a couple of hours or until set.
8. To decorate, place either a paper doiley or a stencil on to the cake and dust with some icing sugar in a fine sieve. Whatever you use, make sure you can remove it easily without disturbing your design!

## Capri Chocolate Cake

*L.D.* When my three daughters entered their teens and life became more sophisticated, this cake became their favourite and they insisted on having it for their birthdays. The recipe was given to me by a large Italian mama at the kitchen door of an hotel in Capri. She spoke no English, I no Italian, but somehow I got it right and it always seems to work. Make the cake the day before, but top it with whipped cream and grated chocolate just before serving.

Serves 10

9 oz sugar
9 oz butter
5 eggs, separated
9 oz ground almonds
4 oz bitter chocolate, grated

DECORATION
10 fl oz whipping cream
grated bitter chocolate

1. Preheat oven to 350°F / 180°C / Gas mark 4.
2. Line shallow sponge tin (11-in. diameter) with buttered greaseproof paper.
3. Cream butter and sugar together until light and fluffy.
4. Gradually add egg yolks. Fold in ground almonds and bitter chocolate.
5. In a separate bowl beat egg whites until stiff, then fold gently into chocolate mixture with metal fork.
6. Pour ingredients into tin and bake for 45–60 minutes till risen.
7. Insert skewer into centre of cake; it should come out a little sticky.
8. Turn out and cool.
9. Cover with softly whipped cream and grated bitter chocolate, and serve.

## Chocolate Bombe

### LOU

This is a delicious and impressive pudding which is simple to make. It can be made days or even weeks in advance and kept in the freezer. Children always love it, but be careful, as it is richer than it tastes!

Use a 3-pt domed pudding basin as the mould. China or ovenproof glass should come to no harm in the freezer if carefully handled.

Serves 6

15 fl oz double cream

1 oz caster sugar

MOUSSE FILLING

6 oz plain chocolate

1 oz butter

6 eggs, separated

DECORATION

grated chocolate or chopped nuts

1. Lightly whip the cream with the sugar and spoon all at once into the mould.

2. Use the back of a tablespoon to spread the cream evenly to line the sides of the mould and put in the freezer to set firm. You may find that the cream slides down the sides of the mould and that you will have to spread it again when it has set a little.

3. Meanwhile, prepare the mousse filling. Break the chocolate into a bowl, add the butter and put over a saucepan half-filled with hot – not boiling – water. Stir occasionally until the chocolate has melted.

4. Add the egg yolks one at a time to the hot chocolate mixture and stir to blend. Remove from the heat.

5. In a separate bowl beat the egg whites until stiff. Using a metal spoon, fold gently into the slightly cooled chocolate mixture.

6. Pour this mixture into the frozen-cream-lined mould and put in the freezer overnight until frozen hard.

7. Unmould about 2 hours before serving. Dip the mould into hot water and ease a palette knife down the inside to loosen the bombe. Put the serving dish on top of the mould and turn it upside-down quickly and the bombe should slip out easily.

8. Before serving, cover the cream surface with grated chocolate or chopped nuts. Use a knife to serve.

A tiny nibble at a time

# *Children's Parties*

*R.D.* I still have vivid recollections of my first-ever birthday party. It was for my fourth birthday, held on 13 September 1920. 'We'll put "fancy dress" on the invitations,' my mother said. 'They'll all love it.' It was decided that I was to be Little Boy Blue because it was my favourite nursery rhyme, and the local seamstress ran up a wonderful one-piece suit with long trousers made from soft powder-blue velvet. It had silver-coloured buttons down the front and a high collar and oh, it was grand! A long hunting-horn was also dug up from somewhere for me to carry so that everyone would know who I was meant to be.

When the great day arrived I, together with two of my sisters (Little Bo-Beep and Cinderella), stood waiting for the guests to arrive. I was in a paroxysm of excitement, and as about twenty Little Miss Muffets and Goldilocks and Dick Whittingtons began pouring into the drawing-room, my excitement and nervousness caused such a ferment within my bladder that the floodgates opened and out shot a stream of pee-pee, like the jet from a pressure hose. In no time at all the entire front of my beautiful powder-blue velvet trousers was covered with an enormous black wet stain that reached right down to my knees. I began to howl and I was quickly whisked out of the room by my mother, who changed me into ordinary grey flannel shorts and a white shirt. 'Never mind,' she said. 'And if they ask you who you are meant to be, just tell them you are dressed up as yourself, because that's what you're going to have to be for the rest of your life.'

Ever since then I have hated children's parties. I think most other children except for the host-child also hate them or anyway find them pretty boring. Certainly they are hell for grown-ups, but, unfortunately, they are socially obligatory, so we must all try to make the best of them.

The problem is, of course, how to keep the little stinkers amused in the hour or so before the tea-feast, and then again after the bun-fight is over. Modern children are too sophisticated nowadays for musical chairs and pass-the-parcel, so all sorts of other diversions have to be thought up. Invariably there is at least one small thug among the boys who needs careful watching and there are girls who weep when they are pinched and nothing is really any fun at all. Some of the wealthier hostesses hire professional party-organizers and these are very talented people. They know a thousand different games and have loud, authoritarian voices, and all the hostess does is to sit back and watch. After tea, a good conjuror or a Punch and Judy show is about the only way of passing the rest of the ghastly afternoon. I even hired an ex-circus woman who came in with a troupe of revolting little performing poodles that jumped through hoops and stood on their heads and then started fornicating together ('Oh look, they're playing leap-frog'). That was a success. But, all in all, these parties are for the birds, ending as they always do with a whole bunch of parents who you've never met before trooping in to collect their by now tired and bad-tempered offspring. And to these strangers you have to offer a drink, which they accept, and so they linger on and you hang around wondering when it will ever end.

However, if we've got to do something, then let's try to do it well, and you will find that our cooks have come up with a few things that are good enough to concentrate the minds of the greedy little bounders round the table and stop them throwing doughnuts at each other.

LUKE'S
BIRTHDAY
PARTY

SHAPED SANDWICHES with various fillings:
cheese spread * Marmite * banana * egg
CRUDITÉS: carrots * celery * radishes
CRISPS * SAUSAGESONSTICKS * BABYBEL CHEESES
CROCODILE
ALLA DAUBE
ICECREAM: VANILLA, CHOCOLATE, STRAWBERRY
ICE CREAM CONES
CARAVAN CAKE
TOFFEE APPLES
LICCY'S LEMONADE

*for Roald Dahl from Quentin Blake 1980*

# Tribute to my Editor

*L.D.* When I went to see Eleo Gordon for the first time, I arrived with my large shopping-bag stuffed full of files and notebooks containing a million mad and muddled ideas of my own for producing a cookbook. I was expecting to receive a polite but cautious hearing; instead of that, her enthusiasm was instant. It bubbled and burst round the room and in a few minutes all my doubts and fears evaporated. In no time at all we were beginning to get down to some serious planning. One and a half hours later, when I hit the pavement outside in Wrights Lane, I had become totally infected by Eleo's enthusiasm. If I had had any sense at all, I would have realized what I was letting myself in for and would have marched straight back in and said forget it. Instead of that, I simply told myself the woman was mad and so was I, and I was going to have a go. I wouldn't let her down.

This enthusiasm of Eleo's sustained me throughout the long process of compiling this book. I didn't find out that her husband was a Russian by birth until half-way through, when I was researching for a good Easter recipe. Knowing that the Russian Easter was a great festival, I asked her if his family had a traditional recipe. 'Yes,' Eleo cried. '*Paskha*. Peter's family have always made it for Easter.' The description was mouth-watering, the method daunting. I expressed doubt about our ability to make it. 'Easy, easy!' she cried. 'It always works!'

I mentioned earlier in this book that we had two photographic re-shoots. This *paskha* was to be the first. Josie took a deep breath. Mould, muslins and ingredients were gathered. Everything you see in the photograph except the *paskha* was poised in front of the camera. *Kulich* made and napkin iced. The moment came for the *paskha* to be turned out of the mould. Upside down it went. Hey presto – a complete flop! I can only describe the result as a white cow-pat. Josie in tears. I rushed out and bought pounds of cream cheese, stuffed it into the mould, turned it upside down and hey presto – it looked perfect. Josie said, 'No, we promised, no cheating.' As always, the perfectionist. Another day and another go and as you can see she was right. So was Eleo. It was easy and I can promise you it is delicious. It is Josie's and my tribute to Eleo for having such trust in us.

*Paskha*

## *Paskha*

Allow at least four days to make.

The word *paskha* means 'Easter' and this is a family recipe for one of the traditional Russian dishes of that period. Its richness celebrates the end of Lent and it is usually served with *kulich* (see the next recipe). A wooden *paskha* mould, decorated with Easter symbols such as a cross, a cockerel or the initials XB, standing for 'Christ is risen', is traditionally used. As this is unlikely to be available, a 8-in.-deep flowerpot (with drainage holes at the base) makes a perfectly good substitute.

Serves 10–12

1½ lb cottage cheese

1½ lb cream cheese

6 eggs

4 fl oz single cream

8 oz unsalted butter

½ vanilla pod, split

2 lb caster sugar

1. Pass cottage cheese and cream cheese through a sieve.
2. Place in muslin and tie up to drain off the liquid. Leave to drain for 12–24 hours.
3. Place cheese in a large saucepan, add the eggs, cream, butter, vanilla and sugar. Mix well. On a low heat, stir constantly until the first bubble appears, then remove from the heat.
4. Rinse muslin and leave damp. Place in the wooden *paskha* mould (or flowerpot), removing as many creases as possible. Place mould over a wire rack (it may need extra support) and stand on a tray to catch the liquid that will drain off over the days. Pour mixture into the mould, making sure it completely fills it. Do not cover the top with the muslin or with the wooden lid at this stage.
5. Place mould, rack and tray in the refrigerator for 12 hours.
6. Drain off excess fluid. Now fold muslin over the top and place the lid on top with heavy weights. Leave for two more days in the refrigerator.
7. Gently remove weighted lid and muslin from the top. Place the serving dish on top, upturn and gently remove the mould and then the muslin.

Serve with the *kulich* decorated with the iced napkin.

## *Kulich*

This Russian Easter cake, made from a rich yeast dough, is served as an accompaniment to *paskha* (see the previous recipe). To bake it you will need a tall cylindrical container or a deep round one that allows plenty of room for the dough to rise. I used an asparagus kettle, which is excellent.

Serves 10–12

6 tsp dried yeast

1 pt milk

2 lb flour, sifted

a pinch of salt

10 oz butter

8 oz sugar

6 eggs

5 tbsp chopped almonds

4 tbsp raisins

½ tsp ground cardamom or cinnamon,
star anise or lemon peel

1 egg, beaten

ICED NAPKIN

2–3 white dinner-sized paper (2–3-ply) napkins

about 1 lb icing sugar

lemon juice

DECORATION

one or more of the following: forsythia,
candied fruits, jelly beans, angelica, silver shot

1. Warm the milk to blood temperature and dissolve the yeast in it.

2. Place the flour and salt into a bowl and pour in the yeast liquid. Knead until a smooth dough results.

3. Cover with a greased polythene bag and leave in a warm place to prove until it has doubled in size – about 30 minutes.

4. Cream together the butter and sugar until light and fluffy. Gradually add the eggs, then the almonds, raisins and spices.

5. Mix with the dough and beat well (the mixture will be fairly thick). Cover, put back in the warm and prove again as in Step 3.

6. Grease the baking container well and then pour in the dough mixture.

7. Cover, put back in the warm again, as in Step 3, for the final proving.

8. Heat the oven to 375°F / 190°C / Gas mark 5.

9. Lightly brush the top of the dough with the beaten egg and place in the oven to bake for about 1 hour. When it is done, it should be lightly browned and a skewer inserted in the middle should come out clean.

10. Cool on a wire rack.

11. To make the decorative napkin, place 2 or 3 paper napkins on top of each other, matching up the folds.

12. Sift icing sugar (be prepared to use a whole 1-lb box for this) into a bowl and mix with some lemon juice until a spreadable smooth paste is achieved.

13. Working quickly and using a palette knife dipped in hot water, spread this evenly over the stacked napkins.

14. With help if possible, very carefully lift and place the iced napkin on top of the *kulich*, allowing it to drape naturally. Allow to set. It is important that your icing is thick, so it sets quickly and is, therefore, 'holding on', not running off, exposing a bare napkin.

15. Decorate the iced napkin with one or more of the listed decorations.

16. To serve the *kulich* lift the iced napkin off and set aside. Slice the *kulich* from the top in rounds. Keep the top slice as a lid to prevent the remaining cake from drying out and replace iced napkin, small children having nibbled the corners.

*Khristos voskrese.*

# *Irma*

## ANN TWICKEL

Irma turned up at Ettal in Bavaria in 1947, a 'displaced person' from Sudetenland. She was well used to being one, as first the Germans and then the Russians had displaced her – all 4 feet 10 inches of her. She proved a natural cook, always ready to try out a new recipe.

In 1960 she came with me to England, where she took over not only the house but also the garden, and really prefers digging, chopping wood and hedge-clipping to the kitchen. Her English has never been perfect and it is heavily overlaid with Czech and Bavarian accents. I keep a list of the words she has invented, which only I understand and are precious to me.

## Irma's Monk in a Nightshirt

### Serves 6

2 oz whole hazelnuts, roasted and chopped

4 oz caster sugar

4 oz butter

5 eggs, separated

4 oz Menier chocolate, grated

4 oz whole hazelnuts, roasted, ground finely
but still crunchy

#### DECORATION

10 fl oz double cream, lightly whipped

1. Butter a bowl and line with the 2 oz roasted
   and chopped nuts.
2. Mix caster sugar and butter, add egg yolks
   slowly.
3. Add grated chocolate and ground nuts.
4. Beat egg whites until stiff and gently fold into
   mixture.
5. Turn into the lined bowl. Cover with a double
   layer of greaseproof paper with a folded pleat
   down the centre and tie firmly with string. A
   double strip of kitchen foil laid under the
   bowl and projecting up the sides will make
   lifting it out easier.
6. Place bowl in a large saucepan ¾-full of water
   and steam for 2 hours.
7. Carefully turn out on to a serving plate. Just
   before serving, pour over some of the lightly
   whipped cream. Serve the remaining cream
   separately.

## Blissful Blackcurrant

PIP

Raspberries can be used instead of blackcurrants, in which case do not use the *crème de
cassis*.

### Serves 10–12

#### BASE

10 oz crushed digestive biscuits

5 oz unsalted butter

#### MOUSSE

1 lb blackcurrants

3 tbsp *crème de cassis*

8 oz caster sugar

4 eggs

10 fl oz double cream

1 tsp ground cinnamon

1 packet (0.04 oz) gelatin

#### GLAZE

4 fl oz reserved blackcurrant purée

1 tsp gelatin

#### DECORATION

a few blackcurrants

1 egg white

caster sugar

1. Grease the base and sides of an 11-in.
   spring-sided cake tin.
2. Melt the butter and mix in the crushed
   biscuits. When well mixed, use to line the
   bottom of the tin. Pack it down well.
3. Place the blackcurrants with 2 oz sugar and
   the *crème de cassis* in a saucepan. Stir over a
   low heat until the sugar has dissolved.
   Liquidize and pass through a sieve. Reserve
   4 fl oz of the purée for the glaze.

4. Separate the eggs and place the yolks with the remaining sugar and cinnamon in a mixing bowl. Whisk until thick and creamy.

5. In another bowl mix the gelatin with a little cold water then stand it in a pan of simmering water until the gelatin is dissolved.

6. Pour dissolved gelatin into the blackcurrant purée and mix well. Fold the purée into the egg yolk mixture.

7. Lightly whip the cream and fold into the purée.

8. Whisk the egg whites until stiff and fold in.

9. Pour over the biscuit base, smooth the top and refrigerate until set.

10. In order to make the glaze, place 1 tsp gelatin in a bowl with a little cold water, then stand in a saucepan of simmering water until dissolved.

11. Mix the above into the remaining blackcurrant purée and glaze the top of the mousse, tilting it to cover the surface completely and evenly. Refrigerate in the mould until ready to serve.

12. To unmould, run a hot knife very carefully around the edges, then release the clip and remove the tin.

13. Decorate with a few blackcurrants dipped in egg white and rolled in caster sugar.

# *Anne*

*R.D.* We had a month to wait before a long-term housekeeper was due to arrive, so an agency gave us two girls for a fortnight each to fill the gap. The first was Josie, the second was Anne. It was an amazing piece of luck. Each of them, one after the other, had the same impact upon the family and I believe the family made the same impression on them. We had never met two nicer girls – cheerful, reliable, efficient, kind, lovely – and, what was even more remarkable, they were both really superb cooks. To cut a long story short, we finally offered them a kind of joint deal, which was this: between them they would guarantee us a full year, working six months each and arranging their separate six months off among themselves. No young girl likes to work a full year living-in in the same house. What they want is six months' work, saving all their money, and then going off to travel and have a good time all over Europe and beyond. The deal was made and everything worked out beautifully. They are both still with us, swapping around on and off, and everyone is very happy.

Anne is a wonderful cook. She learned her cooking on an intensive thirteen-week course at La Petite Cuisine in Richmond and she seems to have learned an awful lot in that time. But then she is a natural anyway, and when she is in charge there is never any fuss or hurry or flapping. Everything goes smoothly along and at the end of it all a magical meal appears on the table. Nothing is overcooked, the vegetables are perfect and Anne is as cool as a cube of ice and still smiling. She has the gift all right and the temperament, and she is always a great pleasure to have around.

## Anne's Winter Fruit Salad

Serves 8

8 oz dried pitted prunes
about 10 fl oz cold tea
8 oz dried figs
about 10 fl oz cold water
8 oz dried apricots
about 10 fl oz orange juice
sugar
2 oz seedless raisins
3 fl oz brandy
8 oz eating apples
1 oz toasted flaked almonds

1. Cover prunes generously with cold tea and soak overnight.

2. Cover figs generously with cold water and soak overnight.

3. Cover apricots generously with orange juice and soak overnight.

4. Cook each fruit in its liquid separately with a little sugar until tender, then boil up the juices to reduce them to consistency desired.

5. Soak raisins in brandy for 2 hours.

6. Peel and slice apples, mix with the other fruits and their juices.

7. Add raisins to the salad.

8. Scatter almonds over the top.

9. More orange juice may be added just before serving if required.

Serve cold with single cream or Brandy Snaps filled with whipped cream.

## *Blackberry Meringue*

JOSIE

Serves 8

5 oz hazelnuts, browned in their skins in a low
oven for 2 hours and then with the skins
rubbed off

4 egg whites

9 oz caster sugar

drop of vanilla essence

½ tsp white wine vinegar

2½ lb blackberries

juice of half lemon

sugar syrup made from: 6 oz caster sugar and
5 fl oz water boiled together for 3 minutes and
allowed to cool

15 fl oz double cream

1. Preheat oven to 350°F / 180°C / Gas mark 4.

2. Prepare two 8-in. sandwich tins: brush with
   melted butter or lard and dust with flour. Line
   the base with baking paper.

3. Lightly crush hazelnuts, leaving them crunchy.

4. Whisk the egg whites until stiff and then
   gradually beat in the caster sugar, vanilla
   essence and white wine vinegar, beating until
   very stiff.

5. With a metal spoon carefully fold in the
   crushed nuts.

6. Divide meringue equally between the tins.

7. Bake for 35 minutes. Allow to cool completely
   before turning out on to a wire rack. Remove
   the baking paper.

8. Liquidize 1½ lb blackberries with lemon juice
   and some sugar syrup to taste. Pass through a
   sieve and pour into a serving jug.

9. Lightly whip the cream until it just holds its
   shape and lightly fold in the remaining blackberries. Sandwich the meringue together
   with blackberry cream and serve.

## *Orange Pancakes*

MANDY DOWN

Marwood Yeatman introduced us to this delicious recipe.

Serves 2–3

ORANGE BUTTER

4 oz unsalted butter

2 oranges

about 50 small white sugar lumps *or*
24 large ones

2 tsp orange liqueur or brandy

PANCAKES

5 oz plain flour

juice of the 2 oranges plus milk to make up
10 fl oz

1 egg

1. Leave the butter in a warm place to soften
   overnight, then cream in a bowl.

2. Rinse the oranges under the cold tap and dry.
   To remove the zest, rub with the sugar lumps.

3. Pound the sugar in a mortar or pulverize in a
   food processor and add the liqueur. Mix into
   the butter.

4. To make the pancakes, place the ingredients
   in a liquidizer and blend.

5. For each one, pour half a coffee cup of batter
   into a pan rubbed with lard and smoking hot.
   Cook over moderate heat to brown the
   underside, then turn and complete cooking.

6. Pile up the pancakes with greaseproof paper
   in between. Leave to cool.

7. Spread each pancake with 1 oz of the orange
   butter, fold in half and fold in half again.

8. Arrange in a buttered dish and place in a cool
   oven (about 275°F / 140°C / Gas mark 1) for
   30 minutes or until needed. Baste occasionally with the melted mixture. Serve.

## Loopy's Pudding

### PHOEBE

We have renamed this pudding in memory of Lorina Crosland (Loopy). It was her favourite pudding and she always asked for it for Sunday lunch in our house. She would lick the bowl clean every time.

Serves 6–8

small loaf of bread

8 oz butter

8 oz demerara sugar

8 fl oz golden syrup

6 fl oz milk

1. Set oven to 400°F / 200°C / Gas mark 6.

2. Remove the bread crusts and cut loaf into 1-in.-thick slices. Cut each slice into 6–8 fingers.

3. Put the butter, sugar and syrup into a frying pan and work the mixture with a wooden spoon on a medium heat till golden brown.

4. Place the milk in a saucepan and bring to the boil.

5. Place the pieces of bread on a plate and pour the milk over. Remove them immediately, so that they do not soak up too much milk. Place them on kitchen paper towels to drain.

6. Now place them in the toffee mixture to coat them.

7. Place in an ovenproof dish, taking care that the fingers do not break up, and pour the extra toffee sauce over them.

8. Bake in the oven 10–15 minutes or until lightly browned. Let the toffee bubble, but *watch carefully* so that it does not burn.

Serve warm with lightly whipped cream. Follow with a long walk!

# Kransekake

*R.D.* Like *krokaan* and *riskrem*, *kransekake* (pronounced 'kranserkaker') is a totally Norwegian food, which every Norwegian man, woman and child knows as well as the British know baked beans and sausages. Happily, it is a good deal more subtle than either of those bland old British stand-bys. It is, in fact, a magnificent many-tiered cake made of ring upon ring of wonderful macaroon-like biscuit, and no self-respecting Norwegian house is without a *kransekake* on the table for the Christmas feast. At Easter they do it all over again, except that the *kransekake* is turned upside-down to make a basket, and one of the larger rings is broken in two to form handles for the basket. Over there they love their *kransekake* so much that it has become a sort of national symbol, which they bedeck with Norwegian flags on these festive occasions, as you will see from the photographs on page 173. A *kransekake* is obviously a bit of trouble to make, but in Norway every mother, sweetheart and cook thinks that the trouble is well worthwhile, and with this I heartily agree. It isn't only the actual taste that is so seductive; it is the aura of grandness this great towering cake gives to the table that makes it so splendid.

*Kransekake*

## *Kransekake*

This recipe requires bitter almonds. Bitter almonds are poisonous if eaten raw but baking destroys the toxins and produces a more concentrated flavour. If bitter almonds are unavailable, then ordinary almonds will suffice.

Serves 10–12

$17\frac{1}{2}$ oz ground bitter almonds

$17\frac{1}{2}$ oz icing sugar

3 tbsp potato flour

3 egg whites

ICING

5 oz icing sugar

1 egg white

1. Preheat oven to 400°F / 200°C / Gas mark 6.

2. Oil the *kransekake* moulds if you are lucky enough to have them; don't worry if they are not available.

3. Sieve the icing sugar and potato flour into a bowl with the ground almonds.

4. Very lightly whisk the egg whites until fluffy and mix into the dry ingredients.

5. Knead to a soft but firm dough.

6. Pipe into the moulds or roll the mixture into $\frac{5}{8}$-in.-thick ropes on a worktop lightly dusted with icing sugar. The small rope should be $5\frac{1}{2}$ in. long and the next 1 in. longer and so on. Make approx 14–15 ropes.

7. Join the ropes into rings and place on an oiled baking tray, allowing plenty of room for expansion.

8. Bake in oven for 8–10 minutes until crisp and golden.

9. Leave to cool completely before removing.

10. To assemble, sieve the icing sugar into a bowl.

11. Add the egg white and beat until smooth.

12. Make a greaseproof piping bag and fill with some of the icing. Snip off the point of the bag. Pipe icing on top of the largest ring and stick the next sized ring on top. Continue sticking the rings together in this way to form a pyramid.

13. Now decorate each ring with a dropped line forming a scalloped effect.

Norwegians decorate the *kransekake* with Norwegian flags and red ribbons tied into bows at Christmas, and with flowers and eggs at Easter.

## *Rose's Cajun Vanilla Bananas*

Serves 4

8 scoops vanilla ice cream

1 oz butter

2 large or medium bananas,
sliced lengthways into $\frac{1}{4}$-in. slices

2 tbsp raw sugar

2 fl oz Grand Marnier,
brandy or dark rum

1. For each serving put 2 scoops of vanilla ice cream in a glass dessert dish and place in the freezer.

2. In a frying pan melt butter over low heat and sauté bananas until translucent, turning once with spatula.

3. Sprinkle with sugar and allow sauce to begin to caramelize

4. Just before serving pour in Grand Marnier, light with a match and pour flaming over ice cream. Serve immediately.

## Red and Blue Fruit Salad with Crème Chantilly

### JOSIE

Make this salad from a mixture of fresh and bottled fruit, the latter preferably in a light syrup laced with alcohol. My suggestions are blueberries, raspberries, black- and redcurrants, black cherries and loganberries.

This salad looks extremely pretty if served in a large shallow white bowl with some of the syrup. Sprinkle with sieved icing sugar just before serving and dot with sprigs of fresh mint.

Serve with lashings of Crème Chantilly *or riskrem* (see p. 176).

CRÈME CHANTILLY

15 fl oz double cream

4 tbsp ice-cold water

3 tsp icing sugar

6 drops vanilla essence

1. Place bowl with water in deep freeze or fridge for 10–15 minutes before using.

2. Add all the other ingredients to the water in the chilled bowl and whisk steadily for a couple of minutes, until the cream has doubled in volume.

3. Now whisk faster until the mixture is very fluffy and forms soft peaks.

## *Riskrem*

### ALFHILD

This is a good alternative to Crème Chantilly with the Red and Blue Fruit Salad recipe.

$2\frac{1}{2}$ pt milk

1 vanilla pod, split

4 oz short-grain pudding rice

pinch of salt

knob of butter

freshly grated nutmeg

$\frac{3}{4}$ oz icing sugar

8–10 fl oz double cream

2–3 blanched almonds, chopped

1. Bring the milk to the boil with the vanilla pod and then slowly sprinkle the rice into it.
2. Leave to simmer for about 1 hour or until rice is tender and most of the milk is absorbed.
3. Place rice in a bowl, add a pinch of salt, a knob of butter, some grated nutmeg, blend together and leave until cold.
4. Sieve the sugar into the cream and lightly whip to the ribbon stage.
5. Carefully fold into the rice with the chopped almonds.
6. Place in a serving dish and leave to chill.

Serve with a red fruit purée, such as redcurrant or raspberry.

## *Gipsy House Almond Tart*

The pastry is best made the day before and is cooked with the filling.

Serves 6

### PÂTE SABLÉE

$3\frac{1}{2}$ oz plain white flour

$1\frac{1}{2}$ tbsp caster sugar

pinch baking powder

$1\frac{3}{4}$ oz chilled unsalted butter,

cut into small cubes

half beaten egg, $\frac{1}{2}$ tsp cold water, $\frac{1}{4}$ tsp vanilla essence, beaten together

butter for greasing

### FILLING

8 tbsp golden syrup

2 oz unsalted butter

4 tbsp double cream

grated zest of $\frac{1}{2}$ lemon

2 small eggs, beaten

4 tbsp ground almonds

$2\frac{1}{2}$ oz flaked almonds

### GLAZE

icing sugar, sifted

1. Sift the flour, sugar and baking powder into a food processor and add butter. Using the pastry blade, whizz around until the mixture resembles fine breadcrumbs.
2. Pour in the egg mixture while the blade is rotating. Work until the pastry sticks together, forming a ball.
3. Reshape, wrap in greaseproof paper and chill in the refrigerator for several hours, preferably overnight.
4. Preheat oven 375°F / 190°C / Gas mark 5.
5. Grease a $10\frac{1}{2}$-in. tart dish.

6. Lightly flour your working surface and roll out the pastry as thinly as possible, but making sure it is still manageable.

7. Line the tart dish and gently remove any air pockets.

8. Now make the filling. Warm the syrup gently, remove from the heat and gradually add the butter a piece at a time.

9. When dissolved, add the cream, lemon zest and eggs. Gradually add the ground almonds and mix thoroughly until smooth.

10. Pour into the pastry. Lightly cover the top with flaked almonds and bake on the middle shelf for about 30 minutes or until the pastry is golden and the filling is set.

11. Allow to cool. Light your grill and allow it to heat up.

12. Generously dust the tart with some sieved icing sugar. When your grill is hot, place the tart under it and allow the sugar to caramelize. (You may wish to cover the pastry edge with some kitchen foil to prevent it from burning.)

13. Allow to cool completely before serving.

# Secret Recipes

## OPHELIA

My sister Lucy and I would always arrive home from school hungry. Dad was often in the kitchen making a cup of tea before going back to his work-hut and he would produce various simple concoctions to keep us happy till suppertime. Pieces of brown toast and honey with thick cream dribbled on top or simply a banana mashed with a spoonful of olive oil, which seemed to intensify the banana flavour. Toast smeared with marmalade and a slice or two of bacon laid on top tasted best of all. As Dad placed the tea-time feast before us he would say, 'This is a secret recipe. A young prince in Dar es Salaam passed it on to me after I saved him from the dreadful grip of a giant python. He made me swear that I would never give the recipe away.' Then he would walk back to his hut without another word. I imagined the royal families throughout Africa sitting down to banquets of toast, marmalade and bacon.

In order to escape the eternal zoom of Gipsy House, Liccy and I made a trip this summer to a favourite antique shop in a nearby village. Among tables, glasses, country chairs and witch balls, I found a leather-bound book called *The Best of Everything*. Published in 1870, it contains lively advice on every household problem, including abstract medical recommendations. I found entries such as 'How to preserve the golden drop plum', 'Parrots and how to keep them' and 'A few words on the preservation of the teeth and gums'. The book also contains an assortment of delicious recipes such as this:

Great Restorative: bake two calves' feet in two pints of water and two pints of new milk in a jar closely covered for three hours and a half; when cold remove all the fat and add a little sugar if liked. Take a large teacupful the first thing in the morning and last thing at night.

As calves' feet can be difficult to find today, I have included a recipe for a scrumptious jam omelette.

# Ophelia's Jam Omelette

For a special treat this is delicious in the afternoon with a pot of tea!

Serves 1–2

3 fresh eggs, separated
a little icing sugar, sifted
1 tbsp milk or water
butter for frying
raspberry jam, heated for pouring
on to the omelette

1. Place the egg yolks in a bowl and beat in enough sugar to sweeten them.
2. Add the milk or water and mix.
3. In a separate bowl whisk the whites till stiff.
4. Gently fold the whites into the yolk mixture.
5. Heat the butter in the frying pan and, when hot, carefully pour in the omelette mixture.
6. When the underside becomes firm, pour a little raspberry jam over one half and either turn the omelette over and serve or, while still in the frying pan, place under a hot grill for a few seconds and it will almost become a soufflé.

Eat immediately.

# Sweet Potato Pone

## ROSE

Serves 10–12

2 lb sweet potatoes, peeled and grated
4 eggs, lightly beaten
16 fl oz single cream *or* milk
4 oz packed brown sugar

4 fl oz molasses

2 oz butter, melted

1 tsp ground cinnamon

1 tsp ground nutmeg

1 heaped tbsp finely chopped fresh ginger *or*
$\frac{1}{2}$ tsp ground ginger

$\frac{1}{2}$ tsp salt

COLD LEMON SAUCE

3 egg yolks, beaten

4 oz sifted icing sugar

$\frac{3}{4}$ tsp finely shredded lemon peel

3 tbsp lemon juice

12 fl oz double cream

1. Preheat oven to 350°F / 180°C / Gas mark 4.

2. Grease a 3-pt ring mould.

3. In a bowl combine potatoes, eggs, cream, sugar, treacle, butter, cinnamon, nutmeg, ginger and salt. Transfer to mould. Bake 1 hour until well risen and firm. Leave to rest a few minutes before unmoulding.

4. To make the cold lemon sauce, combine yolks, sugar, lemon peel and juice.

5. Whip cream till soft peaks form and fold into yolk mixture.

6. Unmould the sweet potato pone on to a serving plate. At the very last moment pour some of the sauce over and serve immediately. Serve the remaining sauce separately.

## Coughton Christmas Pudding

Makes about 4 large puddings. If possible, make these about four months before Christmas, but wonderful if made a year ahead.

1 lb soft brown sugar

1 lb chopped suet

1 lb sultanas, washed

1 lb seedless raisins, washed

1 lb dried currants, washed

8 oz shredded mixed peel

8 oz flour

8 oz fresh breadcrumbs

8 oz almonds, blanched and roughly chopped

8 oz walnuts, chopped

grated rinds of 2 lemons

1 tbsp grated nutmeg

8 oz apples, grated

4 oz carrots, grated

6 eggs, beaten

1 wine glass of brandy and 10 fl oz milk *or* equivalent measure of beer

1. Mix all the dry ingredients together.
2. Stir in well the eggs, brandy and milk.
3. Turn mixture into well-greased basin. Cover each with a double layer of greaseproof paper with a folded pleat down the centre and tie firmly in place with string. A double strip of kitchen foil laid under each container and projecting up the sides will make lifting it out of the saucepan easier.
4. Place containers in saucepans three-quarters-full of water and steam for 5–6 hours. Check the water level regularly and replenish with boiling water if necessary.
5. Reboil for 3 hours on Christmas Day, or day of eating.

Serve with brandy butter made with granulated sugar so that it is crunchy.

## Ginger Pudding

Serves 6

6 oz fresh white breadcrumbs

6 oz shredded suet

2 oz flour, sifted

$1\frac{1}{2}$ tsp fresh ginger, chopped finely

1 level tsp bicarbonate of soda, sifted

2 small eggs

7 oz golden syrup

butter for greasing

1. Grease well a pudding basin.
2. Mix all the dry ingredients together.
3. Beat the eggs with the syrup until they are combined.
4. Mix this into the dry ingredients and place into the well-greased mould.
5. Fill a saucepan three-quarters full with water and place on the heat.
6. Cover the mould with a double layer of greaseproof paper with a folded pleat down the centre and tie firmly with string. A double strip of kitchen foil laid under the mould and projecting up the sides will make lifting it easier.
7. When the water is boiling, place the mould in the steamer for 3 hours. Check water level, replenishing it as necessary.

Serve with some warmed extra syrup and, for real pigs, a jug of cream.

## Curd Tarts

### MARWOOD YEATMAN

During the successful campaign to keep unpasteurized dairy products in 1989 Miss Janet Morris, aged 65, wrote to me from Leeds. Without raw milk, she said, it would no longer be possible to make the curd cakes she had been baking all her life. This is how she does it.

Serves 6

For 1 large tart, or 10–12 small ones
6 oz shortcrust or flaky pastry
1 pt unpasteurized sour milk *or* fresh milk and 1 tsp rennet
2 oz unsalted butter
2 oz caster sugar
1 egg
2 oz raisins (optional)
pinch of mixed spice or grated nutmeg

1. If there is no sour milk heat fresh milk to blood temperature and add the rennet. It will clot and firm up in a few minutes.
2. Hang the clotted fresh or sour milk in muslin overnight to let the whey drain off. The whey can be drunk or used for baking.
3. Preheat oven to 425°F / 220°C / Gas mark 7.
4. Cream the butter and sugar till soft and light.
5. Stir in the curds, the egg and the raisins.
6. Line a greased tart tin with the pastry, and half fill with the mixture. Dust with the spice or nutmeg.
7. Bake for 15 minutes. A larger tart needs a little longer. Eat hot or cold.

## Lori's Apple Pie

Serves 6

7 oz plain flour
1¾ oz caster sugar
3½ oz unsalted butter
2 eggs, separated
2¼ lb cooking apples
1 tsp ground cinnamon
1½ tsp flour
3 oz sultanas

1. Preheat oven to 375°F / 190°C / Gas mark 5.
2. Grease a 1-lb loaf tin.
3. Sieve the flour and sugar together into the food processor using the pastry blade.
4. Cut the butter into cubes, add to the flour and sugar and process until it resembles breadcrumbs.
5. Add the egg yolks to bind the pastry together.
6. Gently knead to a smooth ball.

7. Cover with cling film and place in the refrigerator to rest.

8. Peel apples, core them and slice thinly.

9. Roll out the pastry thinly (but strong enough to survive when taking out of the container) and line the container. Keep the left-over pastry for the top.

10. Mix 1½ tsp flour with the cinnamon. Sprinkle a little on the pastry.

11. Sprinkle pastry with about 10 sultanas, then a layer of apple to cover the bottom.

12. Sprinkle with a little more cinnamon-and-flour mixture, then sultanas and apple as before. Repeat this layer by layer until you fill the container. The apple must rest above the container, as it will cook down.

13. Roll out the left-over pastry thinly, cut into strips and make a latticed top.

14. Lightly whisk the egg whites and brush over the pastry to stick the strips together and to join them at the sides.

15. Place in the oven for 45–60 minutes, until the pastry is golden and the apples are tender (test with a skewer). Leave to stand for 10–15 minutes.

16. Turn out of tin with great care and cut in slices.

Serve with cream or home-made custard.

## Ophelia's Crumble Topping

This crumble was the invention of Ophelia during her keep-fit days. It continues to be cooked and she continues to keep fit.

4 oz butter

4 oz soft brown sugar

5 oz jumbo oats

1 tsp ground cinnamon

3 oz walnuts, chopped

1. Gently melt the butter.

2. Put all the other ingredients in a bowl and stir in the melted butter.

3. Spoon the mixture on top of your chosen fruit and bake for 1–1¼ hours at 350°F / 180°C / Gas mark 4.

## Toffee Apples

### JOSIE

It is best to make these in batches of six, otherwise the toffee cools down and thickens very quickly, making even coating of the apples very difficult.

6 eating apples, washed and dried

1 tbsp water

8 oz caster sugar

2 oz butter

oil for greasing

6 wooden skewers or pencils

1. Put the skewers or pencils in the centre of each apple. Line a baking tray with kitchen foil and grease lightly.

2. In a saucepan add the water, sugar and butter, and dissolve very slowly.

3. Boil to small crack stage 275°F / 140°C. / Gas mark 1 and test using a thermometer. Remove from heat immediately.

4. Dip the apples in as quickly as possible one at a time, and rotate a few times to get an even coating. Place on the greased kitchen foil and leave to set.

If they are to be kept, wrap individually in greaseproof paper, kitchen foil or, better still, cellophane, to prevent them from becoming sticky. Tie with a ribbon.

*Toffee apples*

# PRESERVES AND CORDIALS, SCONES AND BISCUITS

# *Phoebe*

*L.D.* Phoebe has been one of my best friends for the last twenty-eight years. We met as neighbours and shared the experience of being young mothers together. When the time came to write the chapter on preserves I had no hesitation about who to ask for help. It was Phoebe. I have never forgotten, nor have my children, tasting her lemon curd, followed by many jars of jams, chutneys, mustards, etc. In fact, to me she is the example of the perfect family cook – never boring and always delicious. Through Phoebe I met Liz, another culinary expert and, as you will see, a real wizard at the art of jam-making. I thank them both for this wonderful chapter and, above all, for their friendship.

# From the Garden

PHOEBE CAVENAGH

I remember when I was a small child going with my mother to gather anything that was edible from the countryside surrounding our home. We never went for a walk without a basket. My sister and I gathered rosehips and crab apples for jelly. We collected elderflowers in huge fragrant bundles, which our mother would dry and mix with tea leaves.

We knew of a very special mushroom field (our mother was knowledgeable about toadstools and had a lurid book on the subject) and picked all the ones you could eat, all colours, conical shapes and flat ones, including big chalk-white puffballs that were sliced and gently fried in dripping.

All round our home there were large 'Br'er Rabbit' bramble clumps, where the dogs would hunt for hours on end while we picked and picked, gradually becoming more scratched and stained with juice. In our gumboots we braved the nettles to pick the young shoots to eat.

Mother made a vegetable garden on an old rubbish dump, and I well remember the excitement of pulling the carrots and beetroot and discovering mosaics of broken china and coloured glass that were unearthed as I did so. These vegetables, if not immediately used, were bottled and preserved and went to join the rows of jars in the larder. Salt beans, jams, jellies, chutneys, even eggs in isinglass preserved in a huge earthenware crock. These eggs came from a very irate black hen with yellow legs and a few drab ducks called Khaki Campbells, who did not remotely resemble Scottish soldiers, as I felt they should have done.

My sister and I owe our love of cooking and interest in preserves to our mother and her wide knowledge of plants, fruit and flowers.

# Preserves

LIZ

I must confess that I am not in Liccy's magic circle of very close friends but we both share a long and deep friendship with Phoebe, and because of that Liccy and I have known each other pretty well for many years. This and the fact that I am good at making preserves is why I have been invited to contribute to this book.

A long time ago I married a Portuguese baron called Delaforce and went off to live with him in Portugal. When my children were sent back to boarding-school in England, I needed something to occupy me and because I loved making jams I decided, together with a girl-friend, to have a go at starting a small business.

We gingerly made forty-eight pots of all the popular jams, got labels printed, and soon we were ready to sell our products. In no time at all our little cottage industry took off. People actually loved our jam because it was hand-made with loving care, using fruit that we ourselves had hand-picked. There was, of course, a limit to the amount we could produce if we wished to maintain our standards, but as we went along we made a number of interesting discoveries that I feel sure will be a help to all home jam-makers. We discovered that raspberries out of our deep-freezer made just as delicious a jam as the freshly picked ones – in fact, sometimes better in the very hot weather. We found that all fruit could be frozen with no difference to quality. We therefore invested in enough deep-freezers to store a year's supply of fruit, and made jams fresh for every order.

In our small way we were a real success and, dare I say it, the jams we made were really very good indeed. Our little business flourished and over the years I think I learned most of what there is to know about making fine jams and preserves in the home. So let me pass on to you some important points to follow in addition to the basic rules for preserve-making to be found in any reliable cookery book.

To deep-freeze fruit for jam-making just wash it and put it in bags of 2–6 lb. This way the fruit stays absolutely fresh, you can make jam whenever you have time rather than when you are tired after picking the fruit (and what could be nicer than the smell of apricot jam on the boil on a cold winter day when there are no longer any leaves on the trees?), and there is no waste if you have a glut of fruit and vegetables in the garden.

Never make a batch of jam with less than 2 lb or more than 6 lb of fruit; the ideal is about 4 lb.

When stones have to be removed from the fruit, cook the fruit and leave it overnight. Then remove the stones, add the sugar and boil to the setting point.

We made a bag out of nylon curtain muslin for straining the juice out of the cooked fruit; it strained the juices much more quickly than a standard jelly bag.

To test for setting point, remove the pan from the heat, spoon a little jam on to a cold plate and place it in the refrigerator for a few minutes to cool quickly. Push your finger across the jam: if the surface wrinkles, the jam is set; if not, boil for another 2–3 minutes and test again.

Use clean, dry jars, and fill them to the brim, as the contents always shrink when cold.

Seal the jars when the contents are completely cold. I find an inner seal of paraffin wax by far the best way. It does take time, but is well worth it and gives the jam a very professional look.

The advantages of making preserves:

1. You get the most out of a garden.

2. They really do taste so much better than the shop product.

3. The naturally made product is undoubtedly healthier.

4. A varied store cupboard of preserves is always a source of a very personal present: Hot Pepper Jelly for the man who has everything, Sweet Cucumber Pickle for the brother who loves curries, Strawberry Jam for the teenager who wolfs tea-time doorstep sandwiches. Arriving at someone's house for a meal bearing a pot of home-made jam gives me and, I hope, my host or hostess pleasure.

# Three-Fruit Marmalade

LIZ

Makes 8–10 1-lb jars

2 grapefruit, 2 sweet oranges, 2 lemons
total weight about 3 lb

5 pt water

6 lb sugar

1. Cut the fruit into quarters and remove the pith and the seeds.

2. Put pith and seeds in a small muslin sack and tie with string.

3. Liquidize the fruit with the water.

4. Put the purée and the muslin sack into a saucepan, bring to the boil, and simmer gently for 2 hours until reduced by half.

5. Leave this overnight, then bring it back to the boil.

6. Add the sugar and boil until setting point is reached.

7. Ladle into jars, allow to cool and wax seal.

## Apricot, Greengage, Plum and Damson Jams

LIZ

Makes 10–12 1-lb jars

6 lb 8 oz fruit (of one of the above fruits)
18 fl oz water
6 lb 8 oz sugar

1. Put the fruit and water into a pan, bring to the boil, then simmer for about 20 minutes.

2. Leave overnight with a lid on the pan, and remove the stones when cool.

3. Bring the fruit back to the boil, add the sugar and boil until setting point is reached.

4. Ladle into jars, allow to cool and wax seal.

## Marmelada (Quince Cheese)

LIZ

This is a Portuguese sweetmeat that is eaten with a strong cheese from the Azores; mature Cheddar is a near likeness.

4 lb 8 oz quinces

4 lb 8 oz sugar

1. Wash and chop the quinces into smallish pieces, removing the core and pips but leaving the skin.
2. Put into the preserving pan and just cover with water, holding the fruit down with your hand.
3. Simmer the fruit slowly, for about 20 minutes. When it is soft, drain off the water, which can be used for making quince jelly.
4. Purée the fruit. (I use a *passvite-mouli* with a coarse disc.)
5. Weigh the purée. Measure out the same weight in sugar.
6. Return the purée to the large pan and bring to the boil, add the sugar and boil until the mixture thickens, stirring all the time. As it is like an erupting volcano, protect your hands and arms with oven gloves.
7. When ready, pour into 9-oz, deep round bowls and dry in the sun if possible; failing that, a warm cupboard will do.

## Strawberry Jam

LIZ

As strawberry jam is a notoriously difficult setting jam, my version is really strawberries set in an apple jelly. This gives a much better set jam and a far fresher taste of the fruit – a far cry from the dark, treacly efforts of the vicarage fête

variety. I have also used this method with peaches to good effect.

The apple stock is made from good green cooking apples; windfalls will do.

Makes 10 1-lb jars

1¾ pt apple stock made from
2 lb apples
4 lb 8 oz strawberries
6 lb 8 oz sugar

1. To make the apple stock, chop up the whole apples, put in a pan and cover with water, holding the apples down with your hand.
2. Simmer them until they are soft and mushy, for about 20 minutes.
3. Strain off the juice using a nylon muslin jelly bag. This juice is the apple stock and is used in many recipes. If there is too much stock, it can easily be frozen.
4. To make the jam, clean and hull the strawberries and put them and the apple stock into the pan.
5. Bring to the boil and simmer gently until the berries are soft.
6. Add the sugar and boil until setting point is reached.
7. Ladle into jars, allow to cool and wax seal.

## Gooseberry Chutney

LIZ

Makes 5 1-lb jars

3 lb 5 oz gooseberries

2 lb 4 oz soft brown sugar

1 lb 2 oz sultanas

1 tbsp salt

9 fl oz vinegar

1 tsp powdered ginger

half tsp cayenne

2 onions, chopped

1. Put all the ingredients into a heavy saucepan and simmer for 1 hour or until thick and creamy.
2. When cold, put into jars and cover.

## Herb Jelly

LIZ

The timing of this recipe is very important.

Makes 10 $\frac{1}{2}$-lb jars

$\frac{1}{2}$ cup fresh herbs

18 fl oz white wine vinegar

1$\frac{3}{4}$ pt apple stock (see
Strawberry Jam, p. 190)

3 lb 5 oz sugar

1. Liquidize the fresh herbs with the vinegar and put this into the pan with the apple stock.
2. Bring to the boil and simmer for 15–20 minutes.
3. Bring back to the boil again and add the sugar. Boil until setting point is reached.

4. Leave for 30 minutes before putting in jars, as this will allow the herbs to spread evenly in the jelly; they all tend to come to the top of the jar when very hot.
5. Put in jars and cover.

## Sweet Cucumber Pickle

LIZ

A delicious pickle for eating with curries, cold meats and cocktail snacks. It can be eaten straight away or kept.

Makes 4–5 1-lb jars

3 lb 5 oz cucumbers

9 oz onions, peeled

coarse salt

9 oz sugar

4 tsp mustard seed

1 tsp celery seed

1 tsp turmeric

18 fl oz white wine vinegar

1. Slice the cucumbers and onions, sprinkling them with salt as you go.
2. Cover and leave for 2–3 hours.
3. Drain, rinse them with cold water and drain again.
4. Put the rest of the ingredients (the pickle) into a pan, bring to the boil, and boil for 3 minutes *but no longer*.
5. Finally, add the vegetables, bring back to the boil, stirring well, then remove from heat.
6. Put into jars and cover.

## Hot Pepper Jelly

LIZ

Makes 10 $\frac{1}{2}$-lb jars

2 tbsp fresh small red chilli

18 fl oz white wine vinegar

1$\frac{3}{4}$ pt apple stock (see Strawberry
Jam, p. 190)

3 lb 6 oz sugar

1. Chop the chilli, removing the small seeds,
   and liquidize with the vinegar.
2. Put this into the pan with the apple stock.
3. Bring to the boil and simmer for 15–20
   minutes.
4. Bring back to the boil, add the sugar and boil
   until setting point is reached.
5. Ladle into jars and cover.

## Gipsy House Grape Jelly

LIZ

I use pretty unripe grapes for this recipe. There
is a lovely saying in Portuguese when the grapes
change colour, which they do from one day to
the next in the Douro Valley: 'Oh my, Senhora,
the painter came last night', and that was when I
picked the grapes for making jelly.

4 lb 8 oz grapes

sugar

1. Put the washed bunches of grapes into the
   pan and just cover with water, holding the
   fruit down with your hand.
2. Simmer them gently until they are soft, about
   20 minutes.
3. Strain off the juice using a nylon muslin bag.
4. Measure the liquid. For every 1 pt liquid,
   allow 1 lb sugar. Return the juice to the pan,
   bring to the boil, add the sugar and boil until
   setting point is reached.
5. Ladle into jars, allow to cool and wax seal.

This jelly can be flavoured with a small piece of
cinnamon or a clove added to each pot.

## Redcurrant Jelly

LIZ

Makes about 21 $\frac{1}{2}$-lb jars

4 lb 8 oz redcurrants

1$\frac{3}{4}$ pt apple stock (see Strawberry
Jam, p. 190)

approximately 6$\frac{1}{2}$ lb sugar

1. Place the redcurrants and apple stock in a
   pan, bring to the boil and simmer until the
   fruit is soft, about 20 minutes.
2. Strain off the juice using a nylon muslin bag.
3. Measure the liquid. For every 1$\frac{3}{4}$ pt juice,
   allow 2 lb 4 oz sugar. Bring juice to the boil,
   add sugar and boil until setting point is
   reached.
4. Ladle into jars, allow to cool and wax seal.

## Pickled Orange Rings

PATRICIA WHITE

This is a very pretty pickle whose colour and flavour improves cold meat, particularly fowl or game. Be sure to choose seedless oranges; the smaller ones keep their shape better and disintegrate less in cooking than big ones. The recipe is taken from Patricia White's *Food as Presents*.

Makes 3 1-lb jars

8 oranges

1½ pt cider vinegar

2 lb sugar

1 level tbsp whole cloves, heads removed

3 cinnamon sticks

1. Wash oranges and slice into pieces ¼ in. thick. Put them into a preserving pan and barely cover with water. Simmer gently until the peel begins to soften, for about 30 minutes. Take care not to boil hard, as the oranges will turn into a pulpy mass.

2. With a slotted spoon remove oranges to a plate.

3. Add all other ingredients to the water the oranges have been cooking in. Boil hard for 10 minutes and then reduce heat.

4. Slip the orange slices back into the preserving pan and bring mixture back to the boil.

5. Remove orange slices with a slotted spoon and pack into hot, sterilized jars.

6. Boil the remaining syrup until it begins to thicken, then fill jars to overflowing with it, allowing a few cloves, but not the cinnamon, to drift into each jar.

7. Depress fruit with the back of a spoon to release trapped air, top up jars with syrup and seal.

## Lemon Curd

PHOEBE

Makes 1 1-lb jar

1 lb caster sugar

8 oz butter

4 lemons

4 eggs

1. Melt the butter gently into the sugar in a double saucepan.

2. Grate the zest of the lemon, avoiding all pith.

3. Squeeze the lemons. Slowly add zest and juice to the butter mixture.

4. Beat the eggs and gradually add them, stirring all the time to incorporate all the ingredients.

5. Cook gently until the mixture thickens smoothly. Don't be tempted to turn up the heat under your double boiler if this thickening doesn't occur quickly. Gentle stirring and patience is the secret.

6. Ladle carefully into the jar and cover.

# Carvers and Gilders

*R.D.* This is a remarkable story. It concerns four gifted and coura-geous people and I put it in here because it concerns my wife, Liccy. Put very briefly, it goes like this. About fifteen years ago, in the mid-1970s, four people, none of whom knew each other, all decided that they were fed up with the jobs they were doing and enrolled at the City and Guilds London Arts School for a two- or three-year course of Carving and Gilding and Restoration, a fairly esoteric and chancy game, to say the least, and one that could not possibly hold out any hope of riches and small hope of success. These people were:

1. Felicity d'Abreu (Liccy), thirty-eight years old, divorced, three chil-dren, a small amount of alimony but that was all. She had been supporting herself as a costume stylist, mainly for TV commercials. She had no capital. I should mention that I was already in love with her at the time.

2. Bill McCombe, thirty-two years old, married, two children, who had been running a family laundry business.

3. Christine Palmer, aged twenty-five, single, no money, but working in some boring job.

4. Aasha Tyrrell, aged twenty-three, single, a tiny bit of money but not much, and, again, a boring job.

It was certainly unusual that Liccy and Bill, one in her late thirties, the other not much younger, both with children and responsibilities, should give up secure jobs and take this peculiar plunge. They had neither of them done any serious wood-carving before, but they both loved the world of the great seventeenth- and eighteenth-century craftsmen, from Grinling Gibbons to Chippendale, and they must have felt instinctively that some kind of talent was simmering inside them. Nevertheless, it was a mighty brave thing to do. The other two, Christine and Aasha, were much younger and changing jobs was not such a momentous decision at their age. Even so, they too must have felt driven towards this relatively unknown art form.

So the course began and there were about twenty students in all, each of them learning how to sharpen chisels and carve wood and lay on gold leaf by the ancient water-gilding process that involved the use of fine French clays and rabbit-skin glue. And so the months of learning went by, and during those months it became clear to the tutors and, indeed, to everyone else that two students stood out head and shoulders above all the others as brilliant wood-carvers. These were Bill McCombe and Christine Palmer. Either of them could take a block of lime wood and with razor-sharp chisels fashion it into an object of delicate beauty: a basket of flowers, a group of birds or whatever you desired. The other two that are going to concern us in this little story, Liccy d'Abreu and Aasha Tyrrell, could, of course, also carve, but not with the same blazing brilliance as Bill and Christine. Liccy and Aasha's talents lay more in the skilful process of restoration and gilding.

Liccy and Aasha became firm friends over the months, and when the course was coming to an end, they looked at each other and said, 'Well, what are we going to do now?' It was Aasha who said, 'Let's start our own little restoration business.' It was basically a mad suggestion. London already possessed a number of excellent firms that did this work and, as well as that, many of the big antique dealers employed their own people. So how on earth could two students fresh out of art school hope to start up from scratch and compete with these practised experts and earn a living? But nothing has ever been achieved by timidity and nobody could call either Liccy or Aasha timid. They were brave as lions, and they both said to hell with it. Who wants to work for someone else? Let's have a go. They then decided that two of them was not enough. There should be four. So, without the slightest hesitation, they invited the two other people on the course with whom they had also formed friendships, Christine Palmer and Bill McCombe, to join in. They were as brave as Liccy and Aasha and said, yes, by God, let's do it.

But hold on! A partnership of four! That, the solicitors and lawyers warned, would never work. Absolute compatibility would be necessary and this was hard enough to achieve with a partnership of two, let alone four.

The partners all said to hell with that too, and they chipped in £100 each and an official partnership agreement was drawn up. Liccy asked me what they should call themselves and I replied that simplest is always best. 'Call yourselves "Carvers and Gilders",' I said. And so they did. Next, they rented, for very little money, a cold, draughty studio in a derelict chocolate factory in Battersea Park Road and set out to solicit business from a few friends and from the antique dealers of London.

It soon became clear to the trade that these four people not only knew what they were doing but possessed uncommon abilities and flair, and gradually, but not without a few hard times, the little business began to grow. They were never going to get rich, they knew that, because they had to charge by the hour, and the going rate, no matter how skilled the work, was about the same as that of a plumber. The big money in that line of business, as in all the antique trade, lay in dealing – that is, in buying, restoring and then selling fine mirrors and furniture that have been cleverly and, I'm afraid, often deceptively restored. But the four partners, all scrupulously honest, refused to dabble in anything that was the least bit shady.

The long and short of this story is that Carvers and Gilders gradually built up a clientele that provided them with more work than they could handle. They moved to a larger workshop, but it was still only one large room and an office. They took on apprentices and trained them with loving care and brought them into the family. And, of course, they proved all the lawyers wrong, because in spite of all working every day in the same workshop, there were no horrid rows. The friendships not only stood firm, they solidified and fused so that the four became like a family.

Seven or eight years after the firm had started, I married Liccy and dragged her, I'm afraid, away from her work. That was in 1983, but she has never really left them. Bill, Christine, Aasha and, indeed, the whole of the tiny business remain very close to her heart, and she regards herself, rightly, as their kind of mother-hen. She phones

them constantly, visits them often, attends their meetings and organizes their staff outings and Christmas celebrations.

What makes this story so unusual is the heights that these ex-students have risen to in such a comparatively short time. I am not permitted to name the clients they deal with today, but it is a mighty impressive list. Not long ago they were called in to look over the seat of a nobleman whose family was known to have employed Thomas Chippendale himself 230 years ago. There they found, lying around in the dust of the stables and outhouses, amidst the dirt and horse manure, bits and pieces of some of the most precious and important mirrors made by the great master himself. They gathered these bits together. They took them back to the studio and lovingly put them together again and recarved the missing bits and regilded the distressed gold leaf. When these treasures finally appeared in one of our big auction houses, they caused a great stir and fetched prices of six figures for the owner. Carvers and Gilders had, as usual, done the work at the plumber's rate.

But there is more to come yet. In 1989 the final accolade descended upon them right out of the blue. This little group of ex-students was granted the Royal Warrant, and they can now proudly display on their notepaper and invoices and wherever else they wish the royal coat of arms and the famous words, 'By appointment to HM The Queen'.

Every summer Liccy organizes a day's outing for the partners and apprentices, and they always go somewhere that is beautiful. This year they went to Missenden Abbey, which is an ancient monastery on the edge of my own village of Great Missenden. The grounds surrounding the abbey contain enormous and beautiful trees planted and carefully spaced by the monks many centuries ago: oaks, beeches, elms, chestnuts, cedars and especially sycamores. Here follows a picture of the four Carvers and Gilders with their apprentices having their picnic lunch under an ageless cedar in the grounds of the abbey and this is what Liccy gave them to eat . . .

CARVERS & GILDERS
WORKS OUTING

Paella Salad
Mini Baguettes

Beef Royal
Tomato Salad
Lucy's Salad
Potato Salad with Crispy Bacon
Dimity's
Red & Green Pepper Salad

Berry Salad with Crème Chantilly
Selection of Ice Creams
Elderflower Cordial

198

*Bill*

*Bob*

*Liccy*

Christine

Cathy

Aasha

## *Tomato Butter*

PHOEBE

Makes 4–5 1-lb jars

5 lb tomatoes

1 cup vinegar

3 cups sugar

1 small stick cinnamon

1 tsp ginger root

$\frac{1}{2}$ tbsp whole cloves

1. Peel and slice tomatoes, and place in pan with vinegar and sugar.
2. Tie spices in a muslin bag and add to pan.
3. Cook until thick, stirring constantly to prevent burning.
4. Remove spices.
5. Pour mixture into clean hot jars.

## *Tomato and Apple Butter*

PHOEBE

Makes 2 1-lb jars

1 lb tomatoes

1 lb apples

3 cups sugar

juice and grated rind of 1 orange

tomato purée

1. Wash and quarter tomatoes. Wash and slice apples.
2. Put fruit in pan with just enough water to stop it from sticking to the bottom. Cook over moderate heat, stirring occasionally, until tender.
3. Rub cooked fruit through sieve.

4. Measure purée. Each 1 lb of fruit should produce 2 cups; if necessary, use tomato purée to make up to this quantity.
5. Combine fruit purée with sugar and add juice and grated rind of orange.
6. Boil carefully and slowly until it thickens, for about 30–45 minutes, stirring occasionally.
7. Pour into clean hot jars, allow to cool and seal.

## *Rosehip Jelly*

PHOEBE

Makes 2–3 1-lb jars

1 lb rosehips

2 lb crab apples (ordinary cooking apples can be used)

$2\frac{1}{2}$ cups water

2–3 lemons

1–3 lb sugar

1. Simmer the rosehips in $1\frac{1}{4}$ cups water for about 30 minutes, or until soft when prodded with a knife.
2. Roughly cut apples without peeling or coring.
3. Simmer apples in $1\frac{1}{4}$ cups water until soft.
4. Add rosehips to apples.
5. Strain through a jelly bag.
6. Add the juice of 2–3 lemons, depending on the amount of liquid (approximately the juice of 1 lemon to $2\frac{1}{2}$ cups liquid).
7. Add $2\frac{1}{4}$ cups sugar to each $2\frac{1}{2}$ cups liquid.
8. Stir over low heat until the sugar dissolves.
9. Put the lemon pips into muslin bag and tie bag to the saucepan handle so that it is in the liquid. Boil hard to setting point.
10. Put in hot clean jars, allow to cool and seal.

## Pineapple and Rhubarb Conserve

PHOEBE

Makes 5–6 1-lb jars

4 cups shredded fresh pineapple

1 cup water

8 cups sliced rhubarb

juice and grated rind of 2 oranges

7 cups sugar

1 cup blanched almonds

1. Place pineapple in a pan with water and cook covered until tender.
2. Add rhubarb, juice and grated rind of oranges, and sugar.
3. Heat slowly, stirring till sugar is dissolved.
4. Cook rapidly until thick and clear.
5. Add almonds and allow to cool slightly.
6. Pour into clean hot jars, allow to cool and seal.

## Melon and Peach Conserve

PHOEBE

Makes 2–3 1-lb jars

2 cups diced peaches

2 cups diced melon

2 lemons, shredded

3 cups sugar

$\frac{3}{4}$ cup broken nuts

1. Skin the peaches by pouring boiling water over them. Chop roughly.
2. Halve the lemons. Top and tail them and remove pips. Chop finely.
3. In a pan combine all ingredients except nuts.

4. Heat slowly to boiling, stirring until the sugar is dissolved.
5. Cool rapidly by placing pan in basin filled with cold water and ice cubes, until thick.
6. Add nuts and pour into clean hot jars, allow to cool and seal.

## Spiced Pear Jam with Pineapple

PHOEBE

Makes 4–5 1-lb jars

3 lb firm pears

1 orange

1 lemon

4 slices fresh or unsweetened canned pineapple

6 cloves

1 cinnamon stick

1-in. piece of fresh ginger

3 cups sugar

1. Wash and quarter pears and remove pips.
2. Quarter orange and lemon, remove end rind and pips. Place in food processor with pineapple, and pulp.
3. Place pulp and pears in pan. Add sugar and spices tied in muslin bag. Boil gently, stirring occasionally, for 30–45 minutes, until soft and mushy.
4. Pour into clean jars, allow to cool and seal.

## *Cranberry Sauce*

### ANNE

12 oz fresh cranberries

8 oz sugar

quarter pint orange juice

grated rind of one orange

3 fl oz water

2 tbsp port
(I think I probably used 3–4 tablespoons!)

1. Place all the above ingredients in a saucepan over a low heat and stir until the sugar has dissolved.

2. Bring to the boil and simmer for 20 minutes.

Can be made ahead and reheated gently. Delicious served with goose or ham, or even the dreaded Christmas turkey.


## *Gooseberry Conserve*

### PHOEBE

Makes 4–5 1-lb jars

3 lb gooseberries

3 lb sugar

1 lb seedless raisins

juice and grated rind of 3 large oranges

8 oz broken nut kernels

1. Top and tail and wash gooseberries.

2. Mix with sugar, raisins and grated rind and juice of oranges.

3. Cook for approximately 30 minutes until thick, stirring occasionally.

4. Add nuts and pour into clean hot jars, allow to cool and seal.


## *Herb Salts*

### LIZ

Use dried herbs in the following mixtures. Except for lavender, which should be used very sparingly, use equal quantities of all the herbs suggested or more or less of a specific herb according to taste.

FOR USE WITH

| | |
|---|---|
| Meat | sweet knotted marjoram, oregano, basil, thyme, bay leaves, sage, celery seeds, *very small amount* of lavender |
| Fish | fennel, thyme, bay leaves, lemon verbena, lemon balm |
| Chicken | tarragon, thyme, bay leaves, coriander seeds, lemon balm, black pepper |
| Egg | tarragon, onion or chives |
| Salad | tarragon, mint, basil |
| Barbecue | rosemary, thyme, oregano, basil, curry powder, sweet knotted marjoram |

*Herb salts*

## Elizabeth Annesley's Easy Béarnaise Sauce

Serves 6–8

This is delicious with cold fillet of beef or grilled steaks.

2 small onions, finely chopped
4 tbsp red wine vinegar
1 tbsp dried mixed herbs
4 egg yolks
10 oz butter, melted and kept hot

1. Place onions in a saucepan with herbs and vinegar and sweat until soft.
2. Simmer until quantity is reduced to half.
3. Place egg yolks in liquidizer or food processor and beat for a few seconds.
4. Then gradually add half the hot melted butter to the egg yolks.
5. Add the reduced ingredients.
6. Finally, add the remaining hot melted butter.

## American Mustard Sauce

PHOEBE

This is excellent served with fish or hot ham.

8 fl oz milk
1 tbsp cornflour
4 fl oz single cream
2 egg yolks
1 tbsp dry mustard
4 fl oz white wine vinegar
1 tbsp sugar
salt, to taste

1. Bring milk to boil.
2. Dissolve cornflour in cream, add to milk and thicken over a low heat, stirring constantly.
3. Beat together the egg yolks and mustard, and add to the thickened milk.
4. Add vinegar, sugar and salt and let thicken for 30 seconds, stirring all the time from bottom of saucepan.

## Jinny's Onion and Raisin Sauce

This sauce can be served hot or cold and is excellent with cold ham for a buffet meal.

Serves 10–12

4 oz raisins, washed and dried
15 fl oz port
$17\frac{1}{2}$ oz small pickling onions, peeled
(the smaller the better)
2 oz butter
2 oz brown sugar
15 fl oz water

1. Soak the raisins in the port.
2. Sauté the small pickling onions in a little butter until lightly browned.
3. Put the onions, raisins and any remaining port into a saucepan with the brown sugar and water.
4. Bring to the boil and reduce to a liquid of honey consistency.

## Liccy's Lemonade

I invented this recipe when Roald had had a major stomach operation and was very frail, not having eaten for many weeks. It was the perfect solution to getting an egg into him without his knowing it. I recommend it for invalids.

Serves 2–3

3 lemons

3 oz sugar

1 pt boiling water

1 egg

3 ice cubes

1. Grate the zest from 1 lemon, then peel all the lemons, carefully removing all pith.
2. Place the peeled lemons in the food processor or liquidizer, add the zest, sugar and boiling water and mix for 1 minute.
3. Add whole egg and mix for 30 seconds.
4. Strain into a glass jug, add ice cubes and serve in the garden on a summer day.

## Sloe Gin

PHOEBE

This is best kept for a year before drinking.

1½ pt sloes, pricked all over with darning needle

2 pt gin

12 oz granulated sugar

1. Put sloes in a jar and add the gin and the sugar.
2. Cover very tightly and shake.
3. Keep shaking from time to time for 3–4 months.
4. Strain the bottle after at least 6 months.

## Lemon and Elderflower Cordial

AASHA

4 lemons

3 lb sugar

2 oz citric acid

6 elderflower heads

4 pt boiling water

1. Squeeze the lemons and reserve the juice.
2. Chop up the entire lemon skins.
3. Put the lemon skins, sugar, citric acid and elderflower heads into a bowl.
4. Pour over the boiling water.
5. Allow to cool overnight.
6. When cool, press the peels to extract the full flavours.
7. Mix in the reserved lemon juice.
8. Strain and place in sterilized jars.
9. Dilute to taste.

This is best kept in the fridge.

## Fizzy Elderflower Cordial

AASHA

6 elderflower heads (stalks and all, don't wash, make sure they are in good condition)

8 pt cold water

1 lemon, squeezed and then chopped up, pith and all

1½ lb sugar

2 tbsp white wine vinegar

1. Put all ingredients in a sterilized bucket, stir, cover with muslin and leave for 4 days.
2. Strain and place in sterilized screw-top bottles, like those used for mineral water or soft drinks. The fizz will develop in the bottle.

## Mormor's Orange Syrup

10–14 oranges

8 fl oz brandy

2½ pt water

3 lb 4 oz sugar

2¾ oz citric acid

1. Using a potato peeler, peel the zest off the oranges and place in a sterilized screw-top jar.
2. Pour the brandy over the peel, replace the lid and shake well. Leave for at least 1 week, longer if possible. Shake occasionally.
3. In a saucepan bring the water to the boil, add the sugar and citric acid, stirring until the sugar melts.
4. Place the peel and brandy in a large bowl, pour over the liquid from the saucepan. Stir, strain through a sieve, and pour into the screw-top bottle.
5. When you serve, dilute with water.

## Raspberry Cordial

LIZ

Use this as a drink mixed with either water or soda water, or undiluted as a sauce for ice cream.

2 pt white wine vinegar

4 lb ripe raspberries

1 lb 8 oz sugar

1. Pour the vinegar over half the raspberries and crush the fruit with a wooden spoon.
2. Cover this mixture with a cloth and leave for 2 days.
3. Strain the liquid on to the rest of the raspberries, crush again and leave for another 2 days.

4. Strain the liquid again and put into a pan, add the sugar and stir over a low heat until the sugar is completely dissolved.

5. Strain and bottle, and keep for 1 month before using.

## *Pepper Vodka*

*L.D.* This recipe has to be the easiest in the book. It is supplied by my goddaughter, Laura Baker. I'm not sure how it reflects on me as a godmother but there are moments in life you could need it.

Place one red and one green chilli in a bottle of vodka. Leave for a week to a year, depending on the strength of pepper your palate can take. (A lot depends on the type of chilli you buy. They range from very hot to mild, so I suggest you inquire before buying.) Drink in small tots after a hard day. Good luck.

## *Cheese Straws*

### ANN TWICKEL

Equal amounts of:

butter, plain flour, strong cheese, finely grated

1. Mix butter and flour lightly with fingers and add the cheese.

2. Roll out very thin.

3. Place on lightly greased baking tray, indent with a knife and bake for a short time (10 minutes) in a moderate oven (350°F / 180°C / Gas mark 4) but keep an eye on them.

## Mrs MacPhee

ANN TWICKEL

I remember Mrs MacPhee as a tall, rather alarming Scottish woman with a commanding presence, a supremely good cook and the acme of respectability. The only time her sang-froid deserted her was once when my mother, for some reason, took her to Rome on a visit. They stayed at the Hotel Hassler, where the chef apparently went mad one day and pursued her round the kitchens with a carving knife. (Mind you, I would have thought that any Italian hotel-chef who found an outspoken Scottish cook messing around in his kitchen would not only have chased her with a carving knife but would have caught her and finished her off.)

## Mrs MacPhee's Scones

Makes 16–20 scones

1 lb self-raising flour

4 oz lard

1 tsp salt

1½ tsp cream of tartar

¾ tsp bicarbonate of soda

milk

1. Preheat oven to 425°F / 220°C / Gas mark 7.
2. Sieve the flour and salt and work it and the lard together with your fingertips.
3. Add the cream of tartar, bicarbonate of soda and enough milk to make the dough workable.
4. Knead three times to let the air in.
5. Roll out gently to about 1-in. thick and cut into circles with a cutter.
6. Place on a greased or floured baking tray, dredge with flour, bake in a hot oven for 10–12 minutes.

Eat with lashings of Devonshire cream and raspberry jam.

## Arnhem Biscuits

*R.D.* This is a true story about the best biscuits in the world. Liccy and I are very fond of the Dutch people and it is the one country abroad that I agree to visit at least once a year on book business. The Dutch, both adults and children, are avid readers, and my books, much to my surprise, sell almost as many copies there as they do in the UK.

Not long ago we went over at the special request of a children's bookshop in Arnhem to sign books. Holland has lots of bookshops devoted only to children, and the nice thing about them is that they are designed specifically *for* children, with small tables and chairs

and low bookshelves, and they even have some rooms with very low ceilings that only children can enter. It's all splendid. Anyway, off we went to Arnhem and the signing started. The queue outside the small shop stretched like a long, curving anaconda all the way down the street and round the corner into the next block, and the street the bookshop was on became so packed with young people that the traffic had to be diverted.

Liccy, who endures such things with good-natured resignation, sat herself in a coffee-shop directly across from the action and sipped a good Dutch coffee and watched through the window. Suddenly she noticed that a mother and her small son were standing not in the queue but to one side of it, and the little boy was crying his eyes out and the mother was trying to comfort him. Liccy said to the waiter (who spoke English), 'Please go and ask what is the matter.'

The waiter went out and returned and said, 'The mother has to go to work and hasn't got the time to stand in the queue, so the little boy can't get a book and have it signed.'

Liccy said, 'Please go out again and ask the boy's name and which is his favourite book. Then tell them to wait a minute longer.' Once again the old waiter went out and returned and told Liccy the boy's name was Johan and the book he wanted was *Charlie and the Chocolate Factory*. Now Liccy moved fast. She crossed the street and pushed her way through the crush in the shop until she came to me signing away at the back. 'Quick,' she said, 'sign a copy of *Charlie* to Johan.' I did so and, unseen by the mother and the little boy, she carried it back through the crowd to the coffee-shop.

Once again she asked the old waiter to go out. 'Take this book,' she said, 'and give it to Johan and simply say to him, "Now and again in this world something magic happens." ' Through the window of the coffee-shop she watched the lovely old waiter, who by now was thoroughly enjoying the whole thing. She saw him hold out the book with the flyleaf open showing the name and the message and the signature, and she saw his lips moving as he told about magic happening. Then she saw the look of absolute incredulity on the face of the small boy and the gasp from the mother, and the wonder on both their faces as they moved slowly away with the boy still holding the book open in front of him as though it was a holy thing. The lovely thing about Liccy is that she is always thinking up ingenious and surprising things to make other people happy.

But back to the biscuits. A short distance from the bookshop there is a patisserie called Hagdorn at 14 Grote Oord, and while I was still signing away, the proprietor sent in to me a present, a small box of his own special biscuits called *Arnhemse Meisjes*. While my right hand kept signing, my left hand idly opened the box and fished out one of the biscuits. It was flat and thin and oval, and crystals of sugar were embedded in the top of it. I took a nibble. I took another nibble. I savoured it slowly. I took a big bite and chewed it. The taste and the texture were unbelievable. This, I told myself, is the best biscuit I've ever eaten in my life. I ate another and another, and each one I ate only strengthened my opinion. They were simply marvellous. I cannot quite tell you why, but everything about them, the crispness, the flavour, the way they melted away down your throat made it so you couldn't stop eating them. The lady who owned the bookshop was standing beside me. 'They're wonderful,' I said.

'Ah, but they are famous, those biscuits,' she said. 'They are known all over Holland as the *Arnhemse Meisjes*. The proprietor makes them himself.'

'I wonder if you could ask him if he would give me the recipe?' I said.

Off she went and returned ten minutes later with the famous recipe written out by the proprietor in Dutch. It was easy to get it translated when we got home to Gipsy House because Lori, who is Dutch, was our cook-housekeeper at the time. Since then we have made these biscuits several times and although ours were still pretty marvellous, we never succeeded in achieving quite the quality of the ones in Arnhem. But do try to make them. They are well worth it even if you don't quite bring it off. And if you ever go to Holland, make a trip to Arnhem specially to visit the Patisserie Hagdorn, where you can buy the real thing. They are out of this world. Here is the recipe.

## Arnhem Biscuits

ALBERT HAGDORN

We have retained the original measurements of the Dutch recipe. The dough is best left overnight for ease of handling.

Makes about 35–40 biscuits

190 gr plain flour

100 gr milk

4 drops lemon juice (more later if necessary)

5 gr fresh yeast

105 gr unsalted butter (divided equally into 5 pieces of 21 gr each)

a pinch of salt, only if using unsalted butter

rock sugar is used instead of a floured surface (I used sugar cubes that I lightly crushed with a rolling pin)

1. Mix together the flour, milk, lemon juice and yeast, adding a pinch of salt if necessary.

2. With an electric beater on high speed, beat 1 piece of butter into the mixture for about 2 minutes. Continue in the same way for the remaining butter pieces.

3. Wrap the dough in cling film and refrigerate overnight so that it is easier to handle.

4. Preheat the oven to 275°F / 140°C / Gas mark 1 and line your baking sheet with non-stick baking paper.

5. Dredge your rolling surface with the crushed sugar cubes (rock sugar), then roll out the dough over the sugar, sprinkling it with some more crushed sugar and continue to roll until very thin.

6. With a biscuit cutter, cut out the dough. (Ovals are the traditional shape.)

7. Place the biscuits on the lined baking sheets and sprinkle with more crushed sugar.

8. Bake for 30–45 minutes or until crisp and lightly golden.

## Cinda

*L.D.* Cinda is Spanish and was nanny to my children for eight years and to this day she comforts, listens and sorts them out. All their lives they have loved Cinda's cooking and there was no way any of us would let this book appear without one of her recipes. This cake was much loved by them all, especially when dipped into hot thick chocolate made in the traditional Spanish way.

The cake is the lightest of sponges I know. Drier than the Madeira, we often ate this cake warm as we simply could not wait – the smell was too good.

## Cinda's Cake

Serves 8–10

Approximately 6 eggs (must weigh 1 lb)

1 lb sugar

12 oz self-raising flour

a dash of brandy

1. Preheat oven to 350°F / 180°C / Gas mark 4.

2. Grease with oil or butter a 10-in.-diameter high-sided cake tin.

3. Separate the eggs. In a large bowl, beat egg yolks with the sugar until thick and creamy.

4. Beat egg whites until they form peaks.

5. Fold egg whites into the yolk-and-sugar mixture, making sure it is well mixed.

6. Slowly add the flour, beating all the time.

7. Finally, add the dash of brandy.

8. Put in greased container and bake for approximately 1 hour or until skewer comes out dry.

9. Take out of oven and immediately shake out of container, wrap in a cloth and leave until cool.

# Cinda's Hot Chocolate

Serves 2–3

1¾ oz Viso (Spanish) or 3½ oz Bournville chocolate
1 pt milk

1. Grate the chocolate.
2. Place milk in saucepan and heat.
3. Add grated chocolate and bring to the boil, stirring all the time.
4. Boil for 4 minutes.
5. Pour into mugs and serve.

# Easter Cakes

MARWOOD YEATMAN

Makes about 30 biscuits

1 lb plain flour
a little grated cinnamon or nutmeg
8 oz unsalted butter
8 oz caster sugar
3 egg yolks
2 oz dried currants

1. Sieve the flour and add the cinnamon or nutmeg.
2. Work in the butter and mix in the sugar, egg yolks and currants.
3. Rest in a plastic bag in a cool place for 2 hours.
4. Heat the oven to 375°F / 190°C / Gas 5.
5. Roll out dough to approximately ¼-in. thickness and stamp with a glass or pastry cutter of approximately 2-in. diameter. Place on a greased baking tray, with space between each biscuit to allow for swelling.
6. Bake for 8–10 minutes. Cool and serve.

# Zulu Bread

1 tsp instant dried yeast
1 tbsp honey
1 tbsp margarine
1 tsp salt

12¼ oz whole-wheat flour, as rough as you can get (for example, McDougall's Granary Malted Grain Flour and Cracked Wheat)
5¼ oz white bread flour
10–12 fl oz hand-hot water
a generous handful of sunflower seeds, plus a little extra for the top.

1. Grease well an 8 × 5-in. loaf tin.
2. Dissolve the yeast in 1 fl oz of the hand-hot water with the honey and margarine.
3. Mix in the flours, seeds and remaining water with a wooden spoon until the dough leaves the sides of the bowl.
4. Knead the dough until it is elastic, smooth and shiny.
5. Place dough in a loaf tin and cover with a moist cloth.
6. Leave to rise in a warm place (a warm cupboard is excellent) until it doubles its size.
7. Preheat oven to 400°F / 200°C / Gas mark 6.
8. Sprinkle the top of the dough with the extra sunflower seeds.
9. Bake for 1 hour.

Spread with lashings of butter and munch away.

# THE HANGMAN'S SUPPERS

*R.D.* When I was young they used to hang convicted murderers in Britain. There was an official hangman who went from prison to prison to perform the grisly deed, and his name was as well known to the public then as a pop star's is today. Our fellow was called Pierrepoint. You see, I still remember it. And the accepted story was that the condemned man was always allowed to choose his own supper the night before his execution. I doubt many of them chose Beluga Malasol or even Lobster Thermidor, but they did get what they asked for. It was an old prison tradition.

The purpose of this little chapter is to ask a few well-known greedy pigs what each of them would have chosen for supper that night had he or she been in the condemned person's place. It is a joky exercise, but amusing nevertheless.

I'm afraid I myself broke the rules when I was asked to do it, but no matter. That's the way it came out.

A great meal is only fifty per cent great food and you remember it not so much for what you ate but for the person you were with and the ambience and the atmosphere and the surroundings.

In southern Portugal there was a supper in a small empty restaurant on a high balcony jutting out over a deep canyon with the evening sun painting everything burnished gold. Eating alone there with Liccy, in absolute silence, first a plump grilled Dover sole straight out of the Atlantic and with it a bottle of that faintly green local wine that gives off a whiff of angelica when you put the glass to your nose. And the sole followed by an almond tart made by the patron's wife, the like of which nobody has ever tasted before (see p. 176 for our version of the recipe). Put all these small things together and you have perfection which is never forgotten.

Then, again with Liccy, somewhere in France we had a thick slice of poached turbot that was almost raw in the centre but by some magic was piping hot right the way through, and with it a watercress sauce of the utmost delicacy. And nothing else but a bottle of Grand Cru Chablis Les Clos.

Then there was the supper given by my cousin Finn in Norway to celebrate the opening of the crayfish season, with all the family present in the famous restaurant on the top of Holmenkollen above Oslo. The enormous platter in the centre of the table was piled three feet high with dozens of freshwater crayfish caught that morning and you ate as many as you wanted, dipping the tails in plain mayonnaise

made from a first pressing of olive oil and with it a good, crackling cold Alsace Riesling.

In the centre of Newfoundland, which we explored on foot when I was seventeen, in 1933, I fished a small lake that no one had ever fished or even seen before and I caught twelve large rainbow trout. I carried them back to the other eleven of us around the camp-fire and we simply cleaned them and cooked them on the embers. Then we ate them, one fish each, all on their own as we had no other food anyway. The flesh was not pink, it was deep red and for the first, and I think the only, time in my life I realized that wild, absolutely fresh, large rainbow trout has a powerful and subtle flavour. A trout in a restaurant tastes of nothing but the sauce it is served with or the garnish around it and nowadays it is anyway only a pellet-fed creature with grey flesh, but these beauties from the wilds of New-foundland were something ethereal.

The dish that none of my family will ever forget was the ptarmigan that my mother used to bring back from Norway at the end of the summer holidays. Ptarmigan is Norwegian grouse, but it has a more elaborate flavour than its British cousin and when my mother cooked it, always in a casserole (see p. 61 for the recipe), and when she served it with a pale-brown, creamy gravy and small round roast potatoes, it took your breath away.

These are the meals I remember and would like to have again, but, alas, nothing that is superlative can ever be repeated. We must live with our memories.

## JONATHAN CAPE LIMITED
### TWENTY VAUXHALL BRIDGE ROAD
### LONDON SW1V 2SA

Telephone 01-973 9730
International + 44 1 973 9730

Telex 299080   RANDOM G
Fax 01-233 6117

August 7ᵗʰ 1990

Before contemplating what I would choose for my 'last supper' I would like to propose the location. My choice is a Victorian stone cottage I have owned since the age of 19. It is in the Welsh Black Mountains. On a mountain. Surrounded by sheep and wild ponies. This is a place for 'real food'. Please could it be a cassoulet. The ingredients I particularly delight in are smoked ribs of pork (Kassler Ripschen), goose (as opposed to duck) and a variety of spicy sausages. I like the beans to be firm and crispy on top. The dish should taste as if it has been on the go for several days. The starter must not take the edge off my appetite! An oeufen gelée would be perfect. Could the yolk be poached so that it remains runny and the jelly not too thickly set. To finish the meal I would like a lemon souffle. Just plain (no liqueurs) with the top slightly browned and the sides of the dish buttered and coated with sugar so that the souffle sticks to them. And I will make a pig of myself and scrape the sides of the dish. And may I drink a VOSNE ROMANÉE please.

Tom Maschler

DIRECTORS: Georgina Capel  Tim Chester  Anthony Colwell  Peter Dyer  David Godwin  Rachael Kerr  Tom Maschler  Gaye Poulton · Graham C. Greene
Registered in England under no. 195767. Registered office: 32 Bedford Square London WC1B 3SG

*John le Carré*

Dear Roald D.,

First to the menu:

'In the hope that I would soon be restored to the innocence of childhood, I would go for a nursery meal of the sort you can still get at The Connaught: roast lamb + roast potatoes, followed by bread and butter pudding. But I would wish it to be served by a very young, very pretty Nanny.'

How funny that you live in Great Missenden. The first house I owned was a foul little bungalow in South Heath. I wrote my first book on the train between GM + Marylebone. I went back not long ago + there were pixies in the next door garden.

All good wishes to you + your wife.

Best

David C.

*Peter Ustinov*

# THE HANGMAN'S DINNER

My choice of food and drink would not be exceptional in any way. There is nothing like a sense of occasion to make one nervous. I would certainly decline the statutory last cigarette, since the Surgeon-General has warned me that it can be bad for my health. I would also decline the last cigar, since it's slow burning, and only heightens the tension.

I would probably start dinner with a lentil soup, not because it is necessarily my favourite, but because it is relatively rare, and I am always delighted to find it on a menu.

I would avoid meat. On the eve of being hanged does not seem the right moment for carnivorous excess. Fish I would equally avoid, since their remote, cold quality can easily be thought of as sepulchral under such conditions.

A plate of crudités would perhaps suffice to make a more thorough acquaintance of roots, leaves, herbs and weeds into whose realm we all eventually disintegrate. I don't eat sweets (much), but a coffee might be wise

2.

in order to keep my awake.
Why?
I'm an optimist.
After all, I've done enough movies to know that the reprieve will be forthcoming in the last moment, which will allow me to have a *really* good dinner of celebration tomorrow.
But, of course, the authorities may not have read the script.
That's why I have to keep awake all night, planning my escape. You can rely on no one in this mournful world. Make that two coffees. And is there such a thing as a saw in the kitchen?

Dear Liccy

It was a very great pleasure to see you again at the Sunday
Express Awards and I have been giving some thought to my menu
for my last meal.  I am afraid it is rather conventional and
also rather long, but I am unrepentant as I presumably wouldn't
have to worry about putting on weight.

I would like to begin with asparagus with melted butter and to
follow it with melon and prosciutto.  Then, for the main part
of the meal,  I would have roast duckling with sage and onion
stuffing, new potatoes and peas.  This would be followed either ~~strawberries~~ raspberries
by a lemon tart or by ~~strawberries~~ with thin cream, and I would
end with a savoury of field mushrooms on toast.

The most important thing about the meal is that all the vegetables
should be freshly dug or picked immediately before the meal,
**preferably from a garden.**

I am giving some thought to the wines I would drink with the meal
and shall append them to the letter when I have made up my mind.

Please thank Roald for his two letters.  I am relieved that you
didn't actually want a recipe as my cooking tends to be pretty
basic and relies more on luck than on instructions.

With love to you both,

Affectionately,

*Phyllis*

Phyllis White

P.S. I should like
Le Montrachet with the
asparagus - prosciutto and with the
duck either Cheval Blanc 1947 N
Petrus 1961 (why not?)
This is a fascinating subject. An ideal meal depends so much
on place and mood. I might be equally happy with
a Southwold undyed kipper, lightly poached, with
freshly baked brown bread, Unsalted butter, &
washed down with plenty of Indian tea!

*P. D. James*

Best Wishes
Lionel Jeffries

The Chantry,
Bisley, near Stroud
Gloucestershire
GL6 7AQ

March. 25. 90.

My dear Liccy,
      For my "Last Supper" I should like
One pot of best Caviar,
toast, chopped hard boiled eggs,
one thinly sliced onion, and one
bottle of Pouilly Fumé.
      Please send the bill to your
husband my very good friend
Roald Dahl.
      Yours sincerely,
      Lionel Jeffries.

20th April 1990

Roald Dahl Esq.,
Gipsy House,
Great Missenden,
Buckinghamshire.

Dear Roald

Thank you for your lovely letter.

I am very honoured to be part of your cookery
book, but I'm rather shamingly greedy when
it comes to food.  I think my ideal dinner
would be Mediterranean prawns and lashings
and lashings of mayonnaise, proper mayonnaise,
made no doubt, with salmonella eggs, and then
about three pounds of asparagus dripping in
butter and then I'd like lobster thermidor,
because I absolutely adore it and an enormous
green salad, and then probably chocolate mousse
and then I'd probably be sick after that, and
then retire for the rest of the evening, which
I don't think is probably what you want.
But that's what I'd like best.  Maybe if it
was a 'last supper', it would probably finish
me off altogether, which would be a good way
to go.

Lots of love,

Jilly

JILLY COOPER.

May 1990

If I knew it was my last meal,
I don't think I would have much
of an appetite. But since we're playing,
let's say ... mother's milk.
Might as well go out the way
I came in.

*[signature: Dustin Hoffman]*

7 Reec ...
Lo ...
19/12/89.
Dear Roald Dahl
    For my last
supper — I would
like 2 lightly
boiled very fresh eggs
and some bread & butter
Yours very sincerely
Francis Bacon

October 1990

Dear Roald & Liccy:
                    I would like to begin by
cheating straightaway — that is, may my
Supper be a Lunch? If so —

Marinière de Coquillages

A Fresh crab (each) with
                    mayonnaise

Pouilly or Chablis OR (for reasons
of sentiment) Blanc Marine de Pays Charentais

Roast Guineafowl/green salad

Savigny les Beaunes

petits suisses or fromage blanc
                    with cream

Peaches & Grapes

Sauternes or Barsac or Cérons

All this is out of doors and I am assuming
that there are no wasps or mosquitoes. I
shan't mind a few large black bees
bumbling in the Wisteria.
All right?
                    love Quentin —

Quentin Blake

# WINE AT GIPSY HOUSE

*R.D.* Most people develop a number of deep and enduring amateur interests in their lives and become moderately knowledgeable in each of them. My own main interests have for many years been nineteenth- and twentieth-century paintings, eighteenth-century English furniture, gardening, orchids, music and wine. The interest in wine developed first, at the age of about thirty, just after the war, and it has grown stronger with every year.

The late and much-lamented Alfred Knopf, my American publisher in those early days, was the first to initiate me into the mysteries of wine. He was a famous gourmet as well as being a collector of rare wines, and whenever he opened a bottle in his house out in Purchase, New York, and then began to swirl and sniff and taste, I would watch him with absolute fascination. He knew so much about wine and he loved it so dearly that he swept me into his magic circle and I became a disciple.

This is how I first met Alfred. I was living in a small flat in New York and I had just got together my second book of short stories, *Someone Like You*. Both my agent and I were wondering which publisher would be the least likely to reject it. The first book of stories, *Over to You*, had been published in New York by Reynall & Hitchcock, but that firm was now defunct. So we gave, or anyway I was giving, much thought to the problem of a publisher for this new book. Then one morning the telephone rang in my flat.

'Hello,' I said.

'Mr Dahl?'

'Yes.'

'This is Alfred Knopf.' (Alfred told me much later that he never asked his secretary to do the dialling when he was calling up an author. He considered it thoroughly discourteous to keep the other person waiting with a 'Hold on, please, Mr Knopf wants to talk to you.')

I was so dumbfounded at being addressed personally by the most celebrated publisher in America that I said, 'Oh, come on. Whose leg are you pulling?'

He ignored this and got straight to the point. 'I have just read,' he said, 'in my bath incidentally, a short story of yours in the *New Yorker* called "Taste". Do you have any others?'

I told him I had a whole bunch of them all ready and waiting to be published.

'I will publish them,' he said.

'But you haven't read them,' I stammered.

'I will publish them,' he repeated. 'Could you bring the manuscript into my office today?'

That was one Alfred story. Here is another. Alfred Knopf once gave a very grand dinner party at the Commodore Hotel in New York for about forty guests. It was on the publication day of my new book, *Kiss Kiss*, and before the guests went in he had placed copies of this book all around the table, one for each guest. That was a lovely thing for him to have done for his young author. And that, I suppose, was why I was so cross at the cruel and cutting manner in which the French Ambassador put poor Alfred down on the subject of wine. It happened like this. Alfred's wife, Blanche, was a chain-smoker, and while the Mouton Rothschild 1929 was being served and tasted with reverence all round the table, Blanche was puffing away and blowing smoke everywhere. I can remember seeing old Alfred waving a hand in front of his face and muttering, 'How can one taste the wine with all this filthy smoke being blown at us?' To which the French Ambassador replied, 'It won't make the slightest difference, my dear Alfred, after all the vinegar there was in the salad dressing.' Accurate but beastly.

I mentioned that Alfred Knopf initiated me into the real mysteries of wine, but even before that the subject had begun to fascinate me. In 1947 I wrote the short story called 'Taste', mentioned above, which was first bought by Harold Ross for the *New Yorker*. Ross was so bemused by the deep knowledge of wine shown in the story by this young Englishman that he took me out to lunch at the Algonquin with James Thurber. This was the final accolade conferred upon any *New Yorker* writer in those heady Harold Ross / James Thurber days. When Ross asked me how I had gained so much knowledge of Bordeaux at such a tender age, I had to confess that I'd got it all from a book.

'But it's a very complex wine story,' he said. 'How could you have been sure there were no errors?'

'I wasn't sure,' I answered. 'But I was in London when I wrote it and I got hold of the address of the most celebrated wine man in the world at the time, André Simon, and I simply went to his house and rang the bell and asked if he would be good enough to read my story and check the facts.'

'You had a bloody nerve,' Ross cried. 'That man's like God in the wine world. Did he throw you out?'

'He was lovely,' I said. 'He didn't know me from Adam, but he said he'd read my story and told me to come back the next day for the verdict.'

'What happened the next day?' Ross asked me.

'André Simon said, "How do you know so much about wine?" I told him I'd got it all from his own famous book. He roared with

laughter, patted me on the back and said, "No wonder your information is so accurate!" '

Under our house we have a fine large cellar, where the temperature remains constant at about 55°F summer and winter. This is an irresistible temptation to the wine collector. When I started collecting, there were no great wine auctions in London at Sotheby's or Christie's. The only regular one was Restell's. Restell's was a small family firm and they held their auctions every fortnight in the City of London, in Beaver Hall. These Restell sales were attended almost solely by dealers and whisky blenders, but nobody ever objected when a young amateur like myself slipped in and joined the fray. We sat on wooden benches in a vast amphitheatre owned by The Hudson's Bay Co. and used regularly as an auction place for the furs of thousands of small animals. Up on the rostrum the courtly old Mr Restell conducted the proceedings.

This was just after the war, some forty-odd years ago, when import duty was negligible and the craze for wine among the general public had not started. Prices were laughable and you wouldn't believe the stuff I managed to buy there for almost nothing. Good Burgundy and claret could be had for less than one pound a case, and I used to bring the wine home in the back of my old Morris station wagon and fill my cellar with it.

My real love has always been for claret, the wine of Bordeaux. There is a mystique about good claret, a kind of magic aura that no other wine in the world possesses. Mysterious changes take place in the fruits and tannins while the bottle is resting quietly in your cellar over the years. Often the wine will remain closed up and aloof for a decade or more, and all the while some secret chemistry is slowly converting it into a glorious and complex nectar. Also, the way the stuff opens up after being poured into the glass, sometimes taking ten or twenty minutes to do so, is astonishing. It is matters such as these that fascinate the lover of claret.

Now, in my advancing years and with a bit more money to spend, I have been slowly collecting and laying down some very good wines. The 1959s and the '61s and '70s have all been drunk, but luckily I went banco on the 1982s and bought about 1,000 cases of this tremendous vintage *en primeur*, when the wine was still in the cask and the prices were reasonable. The American wine writer Robert Parker was the first to alert me to the greatness of the '82 vintage, but because the grapes had only just been pressed and put in the cask, I was wary about relying on one man's advice. So I called up my friend Bruno Prats, owner of the fine second-growth Château Cos d'Estournel, to double check. Bruno told me on the phone that his 1982 was the best wine he had ever made and predicted that this was going to be one of the vintages of the century.

So I gave my enormous order of 1,000 cases to one of the *en primeur* merchants and was happy to put the money down immediately despite the fact that the wine would not reach me for two years. The 1982s that I bought were:

> Mouton Rothschild
> La Fleur
> Cos d'Estournel
> Leoville Les Cases
> Pichon Longueville Lalande
> La Mission Haut Brion
> Certain de May
> Leoville Barton
> Canon
> Branaire Ducru

and then some *cru bourgeois*:

> De Sales
> L'Angelus
> Beauregard
> Du Tailhas

The way down to our cellar is long and steep, and it is no joke to totter down there carrying a full case of wine. So before my 1,000 cases of 1982 arrived, I had a carpenter make a wooden chute down which the cases could be slid. This made things a lot easier when the large consignment arrived at last from France.

Most of these great 1982s are still maturing in the cellar, and most of the bigger wines will not be ready to drink until 1995 or 2000. But the *cru bourgeois* are already delicious and we drink them all the time. Occasionally, we steal a bottle of one of the greats, and it is intriguing to monitor from month to month how the wine is constantly changing, how the tannins are becoming less evident and the gorgeous fruit is gradually taking over. I realize very well how lucky I am to be able to 'play' with great wines in this way. But it had nothing to do with my own cleverness. I simply took the advice of inspired experts and was willing to spend a large part of my savings on this lovely hobby.

No evening meal is ever eaten at Gipsy House without wine. As the years go by and the great '82s become fully mature, it will be wonderful to drink them freely in the knowledge that they cost so little when they were bought long ago. That is the fine thing about good Bordeaux: it will always last for your lifetime. And, I'm afraid, in my case, many years longer. Fine claret, like vintage port and the planting of trees, can be a gift to one's grandchildren.

# DOGS' DINNERS

*R.D.*   We would like to end the family cookbook with a few recipes and comments from our four-legged family, Eva, aged seventeen, and Chopper, aged four and a half, their cousins and their great friend, Heidi. The following Distinguished Dogs' Diet is written by my niece Atty, a great lover of all animals, especially her dogs.

## *Distinguished Dogs' Diet*

ATTY NEWMAN

1. Stripping carefully cultivated and cherished rows of peas ... Taking, secretly, tender and most precious asparagus tips – leaving the tough ones for us. ...

2. Slimming human consumption (and preferably organic) meat stew. Devised by honorary dietitian (Alfhild):

3. Handful of traditional Vitalin.

4. Pip's special diet for pancreas troubles of old age (which causes dog-style hysteria) is a small daily blob of poly-unsaturated spread for dry and lifeless coats.

5. And no chocolates – unlike the Dahls' dogs!

We (humans and animals) realize how lucky we are to eat well each day, so we regularly subscribe to charitable organizations for less fortunate humans and animals at home and abroad.

*Chopper and Eva outside the summerhouse*

## *Undistinguished Dogs' Diet*

*R.D.* Now in comes the riot squad – Eva, Chopper and Heidi.

The dogs who inhabit our house subscribe to the same philosophy about food as do the humans. If something is delicious – for example, chocolate – then they (and we) eat it and enjoy it and to hell with the consequences. Our dogs take the view that, anyway, life is short and you might as well make the most of it while you have the chance. Our dogs believe that mealtimes are the most pleasurable moments of life. They are not allowed to beg at table, but the moment lunch and supper are over they advance for their ration of Smarties, four for Chopper and six for Eva. The digestive biscuit on the bean-bag last thing at night is another high point and Chopper in particular becomes almost hysterical with anticipation as the biscuit is brought forward. One must remember that dogs have fewer mealtimes than we do and therefore when the moment of eating arrives, it is all the more exciting. It is my view that dogs get an even greater kick out of eating than pigs like us.

The large dog in the picture is Heidi, who has become a close friend of both Chopper and Eva during the making of this book. She belongs to Jan, the great photographer, and has spent hundreds of hours here as a welcome visitor, always charming, quiet and well behaved, which is more than I can say for our own revolting but lovable creatures.

*Eva, Heidi and Chopper*

# SUPPLIERS

### CRAFTSMEN

Carvers and Gilders, Charterhouse Works, Unit 9, Eltringham Street, London SW18 1TD, Tel: (0181) 870 7047

### LETTER CARVERS AND SCULPTORS

Fiona and Alec Peever, The Old Post Office, Coombe, Oxon. OX7 2NA, Tel: (01993) 898397

### VEGETABLE SEEDS

W. Robinson and Sons Ltd, Sunny Bank, Forton, Near Preston, Lancs. PR5 0BN, Tel: (01524) 791219

### GAME

William Fison, Elmsett Game Farm, Little Greys, Great Cornard, Sudbury, Suffolk CO10 0QD, Tel: (01787) 74580

### HAMS, BACON, ETC.

Richard Woodall, Lane End, Waberthwaite, Near Millom, Cumbria LA19 5YJ, Tel: (01229 717) 237

### FRUIT

Williamson's Fruit Farms Ltd, Park Lane Farm, Langham, Essex, CO4 5NL, Tel. (01206) 230233

### DRIED FRUIT AND NUTS

Neal's Yard, 21 Shorts Gardens, London WC2H 9DP, Tel: (0171) 836 5151

### BUTCHERS

W. Lacy, 4 Banks Parade, Haddenham, Bucks. HP17 8ED, Tel. (01844) 291332

Hopper and Babb, 101 Sycamore Road, Amersham, Bucks. HP6 5EJ, Tel: (01494) 727997

M. Newitt & Sons, 10 High Street, Thame, Oxon OX9 2BZ, Tel: (01844) 212103

### THAI FOOD SUPPLIERS

Tawana Oriental Supermarket, 18–20 Chepstow Road, London W2 5BD, Tel: (0171) 221 6316

### WHOLESALE FOOD

Larder Fresh, 13 Bermondsey Trading Estate, Rotherhithe New Road, London SE16 3LL, Tel: (0171) 231 9911

FOOD-GRADE WAX FOR JAM JARS

Candle Makers Suppliers, 28 Blythe Road, London W14 0HA, Tel: (0171) 602 4031

KITCHEN EQUIPMENT

David Shuttle, 9 The Broadway, Beaconsfield, Bucks. HP9 2PA, Tel: (01494) 677665

David Mellor, 4 Sloane Square, London SW1W 8EE, Tel: (0171) 730 4259

CHEESES

Jeroboams, who have three branches at: 26 Bute Street, London SW7 3EX, Tel: (0171) 225 2232, 51 Elizabeth Street, London SW1 W9PP, Tel: (0171) 823 5623 and 6 Clarendon Road, London W11 3AA, Tel: (0171) 727 9359

FLOWERS

David Jones and Noel Minnett, 108a Bishops Road, London SW6 7AU, Tel: (0181) 870 4394

House of Flowers, 91 High Street, Prestwood, Bucks. HP16 9ER, Tel: (01494) 865401

# CONVERSION TABLES

The conversions in the following tables are not always exact, but are rounded off for convenience and practicality.

## *Solids*

| IMPERIAL | METRIC | IMPERIAL | METRIC | IMPERIAL | METRIC | IMPERIAL | METRIC |
|---|---|---|---|---|---|---|---|
| $\frac{1}{4}$ oz | 8 g | $3\frac{1}{2}$ oz | 100 g | $8\frac{1}{2}$ oz | 240 g | 16 oz/1 lb | 450 g |
| $\frac{1}{2}$ oz | 15 g | 4 oz | 115 g | 9 oz | 255 g | $1\frac{1}{4}$ lb | 565 g |
| $\frac{3}{4}$ oz | 20 g | $4\frac{1}{2}$ oz | 130 g | $9\frac{1}{2}$ oz | 270 g | $1\frac{1}{2}$ lb | 675 g |
| 1 oz | 25–30 g | 5 oz | 140 g | 10 oz | 285 g | $1\frac{3}{4}$ lb | 790 g |
| $1\frac{1}{4}$ oz | 35 g | $5\frac{1}{2}$ oz | 155 g | $10\frac{1}{2}$ oz | 300 g | 2 lb | 900 g |
| $1\frac{1}{2}$ oz | 45 g | 6 oz | 170 g | 11 oz | 315 g | $2\frac{1}{4}$ lb | 1 kg |
| $1\frac{3}{4}$ oz | 50 g | $6\frac{1}{2}$ oz | 185 g | 12 oz | 340 g | $2\frac{1}{2}$ lb | 1.1 kg |
| 2 oz | 55 g | 7 oz | 200 g | 13 oz | 370 g | 3 lb | 1.4 kg |
| $2\frac{1}{2}$ oz | 70 g | $7\frac{1}{2}$ oz | 215 g | 14 oz | 400 g | 4 lb | 1.8 kg |
| 3 oz | 85 g | 8 oz | 225 g | 15 oz | 425 g | 5 lb | 2.25 kg |
| | | | | | | 6 lb | 2.7 kg |

## *Liquids*

| IMPERIAL | METRIC | IMPERIAL | METRIC | IMPERIAL | METRIC | IMPERIAL | METRIC |
|---|---|---|---|---|---|---|---|
| 1 tsp | 5 ml | 4 fl oz | 115 ml | 10 fl oz | 285 ml | 16 fl oz | 455 ml |
| 1 tbsp | 15 ml | 5 fl oz | 145 ml | 11 fl oz | 315 ml | 17 fl oz | 485 ml |
| $\frac{1}{2}$ fl oz | 15 ml | 6 fl oz | 170 ml | 12 fl oz | 340 ml | 18 fl oz | 510 ml |
| 1 fl oz | 30 ml | 7 fl oz | 200 ml | 13 fl oz | 370 ml | 19 fl oz | 540 ml |
| 2 fl oz | 55 ml | 8 fl oz | 225 ml | 14 fl oz | 400 ml | 20 fl oz | 570 ml |
| 3 fl oz | 85 ml | 9 fl oz | 255 ml | 15 fl oz | 425 ml | | |

## *Distance*

| IMPERIAL | METRIC | IMPERIAL | METRIC | IMPERIAL | METRIC | IMPERIAL | METRIC |
|---|---|---|---|---|---|---|---|
| $\frac{1}{4}$ in | 6 mm | 2 in | 5 cm | 6 in | 15 cm | 10 in | 25 cm |
| $\frac{1}{2}$ in | 1 cm | 3 in | 7.5 cm | 7 in | 18 cm | 11 in | 28 cm |
| $\frac{3}{4}$ in | 2 cm | 4 in | 10 cm | 8 in | 20 cm | 12 in | 30 cm |
| 1 in | 2.5 cm | 5 in | 12.5 cm | 9 in | 23 cm | | |

# ACKNOWLEDGEMENTS

## *The Cooks*

We thank the following members and friends of our family for the delicious recipes they have contributed to this book. You will be aware of them only by their first names placed above their recipes. We are therefore now giving you their surnames.

## *The family*

Tessa Dahl, Sophie Holloway, Ophelia Dahl, Theo Dahl, Lucy and Michael Faircloth, Neisha Barranco, Charlotte Crosland, Spiv and Marius Barran, Ann Twickel, Clare McLaren, Else Logsdail, Alfhild Hansen, Astri Newman, Asta Anderson, Lou Pearl, Anna Corrie, Rose Holbrook.

## *Friends*

Quentin Blake, Marwood Yeatman, Pip Hickmott, Phoebe Cavenagh, Liz Delaforce, Cinda Perez, Anne Bird, Callie Hope-Morley, Sandy Andersen, Virginia Johnson, Sarah Freeth, Lori Wijnnobel, Kathy Tully, Ali Watkinson, Mr Wells, Irma, Jennifer Neelands, Virginia Ash, Fran Collins, Dimity Huntingdon, Marianne Ford, Penny Minto, Liz Annesley, Aasha Tyrrell, Priscilla Berens, Laura Baker, Ruth Parish, Jinny Ash, Peter Carson.

## *The pros*

We would also like to thank the real professionals who have kindly let us include their recipes in this book, recipes that we constantly use and enjoy.
Arabella Boxer, François Clerc, Jane Grigson, Albert Hagdorn, Prue Leith, Delia Smith, Richard Stein, Patricia H. White.

# *Personal thanks*

We are deeply grateful to the following:

Quentin Blake for giving us a family tree to be handed down in perpetuity to future generations.

Wendy Kress, our scrumdiddlyumptious secretary, who has never stopped typing, retyping and re-retyping the entire contents of this book. A mammoth task.

Cathy Sinker for all her creative styling in Jan's photographs.

Jo Stilwell, Jan's patient, reliable assistant and photographer of all the cut-out pictures.

Fiona and Alec Peever's beautifully written menus.

Keith Pounder, our gardener, who has created our walled vegetable garden and supplied us with its delicious contents.

The Bedfords at Town Farm for their fresh farmyard eggs.

Professor Potts the Clown (Graham Nichols: 7 Lowden, Chippenham, Wiltshire, SN15 2BS, tel: (01249) 657419) for his patience and loving way of handling a bunch of wild children at Luke's party.

Our entire family and friends who have donated the recipes for this book for the tolerance they have shown in tasting and retasting and the chaos that Josie and Liccy have caused at Gipsy House.

And for giving us their grounds for our works outing:

The Missenden Abbey Management Centre, Great Missenden, Bucks. Tel: (01494) 866811

# INDEX